TRUMAN CAPOTE

Children on Their Birthdays

Reading a Truman Capote Short Story

詳注詳解
カポーティの「誕生日の子どもたち」

edited with notes by
KAREN MCGEE
KEIICHIRO UETSUKI
MEGUMI MATSUURA

JN034084

TSURUMI SHOTEN

自習用音声について

本書の自習用音声は以下よりダウンロードできます。予習、復習にご利用ください。
（2023 年 4 月 1 日開始予定）

http://www.otowatsurumi.com/0057/

URL はブラウザのアドレスバーに直接入力して下さい。

まえがき

外国語を知らない人は、自国語について何も知らない。（ゲーテ）

『日本人は英語をどう学んできたか——英語教育の社会文化史』（研究社、2008）でも有名な江利川春雄氏の『英語教育論争史』（講談社、2022 年 9 月）が、話題になっています。昭和50 年頃の平泉渉氏と渡部昇一氏の大論争を思い出さずにはいられませんが、立場はどうあれ、次の事実におそらく変わりはないでしょう。

　　大學時代は有効に語学に費やし得らるる殆ど最後の時期である事を心に銘して戴き度い。（市河三喜『昆虫・言葉・國民性』研究社出版、昭和 14 年、152 頁）

インターネット、デジタル、AI の時代で、やる気さえあれば、就職してからでも語学の勉強は可能でしょう。でも、20 歳前後の多感な時期に精神的栄養たっぷりのものをしっかりと咀嚼して読み込んでおくことは、その人の生涯の大きな支えになると思います。

というわけで、学生読者諸氏が感情移入もしやすいように、中高生くらいから社会へ飛躍するちょうど間の時期を捉え、筋の展開も面白く、何よりも誰もが持っている「誕生日」が大きなテーマの一つである「誕生日の子どもたち」(*Children on Their Birthdays*, 1948 by Truman Capote) を選び、それに詳細な注と解説、さらには練習問題を付けました。

言語には感情が伴うし、体験を伴ってこそ身につくものでしょう。青春ものとはいえ、大学生からすれば、さらに 5，6 年幼い年齢になりますが、その少年少女たちのアメリカ南部を追体験してもらいたいと思います。

タイトルの「誕生日の子どもたち」(children on their birthdays) という語句は、全部で 26段落あるうちの、ちょうど真ん中辺り第 13 段落に記してあり、女性主人公のボビット嬢が次のように語る一節に含まれています。

　　I think always about somewhere else, somewhere else where everything is dancing, like people dancing in the streets, and everything is pretty, like children on their birthdays.

誕生日はふつう誰でも心が弾むものです。幼いころの誕生日には、思わず踊りだしたくなるような、すべてが魅力的に見え、何かしらキラキラ輝いていた、そんなときではなかったでしょうか。誕生日は毎年訪れるし、その度にあのころを思い出し、この世に生まれてきた意味を考えながら読んでいくのもいいと思います。

否、むしろ birthday ではなく、un-birthday を、つまりルイス・キャロル (Lewis Carroll) の『鏡の国のアリス』(*Through the Looking-Glass, and What Alice Found There*, 1871) での会話 'What is an un-birthday present?' 'A present given when it isn't your birthday, of course.' を思い出し、いわゆる誕生日以外の 364 日に思いを馳せてみてもいいかもしれません。教員も学生も、中学生くらいの自分を思い出しながら、英語学習に勤しんでもらったらよいのではないかと思います。

主人公のボビット嬢について言えば、オードリー・ヘップバーン主演の映画《ティファニーで朝食を》(*Breakfast at Tiffany's*, 1961) のホリー・ゴライトリーに発展するキャラクターと言われます。この映画を鑑賞したり、有名な挿入歌《ムーン・リバー》("Moon River") を口ずさんでみるのもいいでしょう。さらに余力があれば、その原作、カポーティの『ティファニーで朝食を』(*Breakfast at Tiffany's*, 1958) を原文で部分的にでも味読してもいいと思います。

音の芸術や色の芸術に触れることは推奨されます。言語芸術の一形式である小説を教材にする是非については、いろいろ議論もあるでしょうが、やはりそれに触れて徹底的に精読してもよいと思います。そこには、単なるエッセイなどとも異なる香り豊かな地の文がありますし、血の通った人間同士の感情の陰翳を感じられる味わい深い会話があります。問題は訳読で終わってしまいがちなところです。

本作にはすでに翻訳はありますが、単なる訳読で終わらないように、豊富な練習問題を、易しいものを数多くという方針で用意しました。苦手な学生は、日常の日本語の領域から授業の中の英語の領域に移るだけで大変な苦労をする場合もあるので、各ユニットの最初に、そのユニットの冒頭に近い語句を使った例文を音読する Warm Up を設けました。

音読は重要です。よく英語教育批判として、10 年やったけど全然話せるようにはならなかったなどと言われます。しかし、その人は、少なくとも英語の時間にどれだけ英語を喋ったでしょうか。言語の大原則ですが、喋ったこともないことばを喋れるようにはなりません。

習熟度の高い学生のために、作家であり元日本大学教授のカレン・ミギー (Karen McGee) 氏お勧めの方法論、小説を教材とした発展学習を TM の方で紹介しています。彼女の短編 "Dot Rat" は、*Best American Mystery Stories 2017* (Mariner Books, 2017) に収録されているので、併せてそちらもご一読いただければ幸いです。彼女には各ユニットの要約文や最後の定期試験問題も作成してもらっています。全体的にも目を通して頂き、お礼申し上げます。

対注もスペースの関係で必要最小限でしかありません。今はネットで無料の辞書もたくさんあり、たとえば、onelook.com などの英英辞典も含め、その定義と用例にはたくさん当たってもらいたいと思います。辞書の意味を確認すると、定義 definition というが如しで、ある得体のしれないものをきちんと言語で把握する力を養ってくれます。人文科学の α であり ω であるのが事典辞書類です。柔道選手の受け身の如しで、繰り返し consult することでどんどん実力がつくはずです。

最後になりましたが、注を付けるにあたって、堅実な注はもちろんですが、全体計画の策定、作業用の Google drive の設定、リモートでの打ち合わせなどを担当してくれた松浦恵美日本大学芸術学部専任講師にはこの場を借りてお礼申し上げます。

登場人物イラストも本書の大きな特徴です。作品理解に欠かせないイメージを提供していただきました。表紙も含め、人とハートを重ね合わせた日本大学芸術学部デザイン学科助手である田中希実さんの作品です。感謝申し上げます。

2022 年 11 月

植 月　惠一郎

＊参考辞書

『コンパスローズ英和辞典』赤須薫編、研究社、2018.11.
『新英和大辞典』竹林滋編集代表、研究社、2006.9、第 6 版.
『新英和中辞典』竹林滋（ほか）編、研究社、2003.4、第 7 版.
『リーダーズ・プラス』松田徳一郎監修、研究社、2000.2.
『ランダムハウス英和大辞典』小学館ランダムハウス英和大辞典第二版編集委員会編、小学館、
　　1994.1、第 2 版.

トルーマン・カポーティについて

　トルーマン・カポーティ (Truman Capote) は 1924 年、アメリカ南部のルイジアナ州ニューオリンズに生まれました。両親は幼いころに離婚し、トルーマンはルイジアナ州、ミシシッピー州、アラバマ州の親戚の家を転々としながら、不安定な少年時代を過ごします。1945 年に短編小説「ミリアム」("Miriam")、「夜の樹」("A Tree of Night") を発表し、若き天才作家の登場として注目を集めます。その後、1948 年に長編小説『遠い声、遠い部屋』(Other Voices, Other Rooms) を出版、こちらも大きな反響を呼び、一躍時代の寵児となります。

　カポーティの作品はいくつかの異なるスタイルにわけられるでしょう。ひとつは、彼が幼少期を過ごした南部を舞台とした作品です。その中でも、「夜の樹」や『遠い声、遠い部屋』のように、ミステリアスでゴシック的な世界観を持つ作品もあれば、『草の竪琴』(The Grass Harp, 1951) や「クリスマスの思い出」("A Christmas Memory," 1956) のように、いとこたちと過ごしたあたたかい日々を描いた作品もみられます。また、ニューヨークを舞台とした『ティファニーで朝食を』(Breakfast at Tiffany's, 1958) に代表されるような、大都会やセレブリティたちの集う社交界を描いた作品もあります。『ティファニーで朝食を』はオードリー・ヘプバーン主演で映画化され、大ヒットを収めました。1966 年に発表された『冷血』(In Cold Blood) は、カンザス州で実際に起きた殺人事件を丹念に取材した「ノンフィクション・ノヴェル」であり、カポーティが新たな表現に挑戦した作品でもありました。しかし、『冷血』出版後は創作上の困難、社交界の友人たちからの反発などから私生活も乱れ、1984 年、心臓発作で急死します。

　「誕生日の子どもたち」("Children on Their Birthdays," 1949) は、カポーティの幼少期のあたたかい思い出を反映した作品です。アラバマ州の田舎町を舞台に、地元の子どもたちと、この町に突然現れたミス・ボビット (Miss Bobbit) という魅力的で個性的な少女の物語が、南部の文化を背景に展開されます。ここには、南部の田舎町の素朴な人々、その保守的な慣習、またミス・ボビットの自由さ、そして、過ぎ去っていく子ども時代のはかなさなどが描かれています。

松浦　恵美

CONTENTS

Children on Their Birthdays

—— 登場人物 ——
Characters

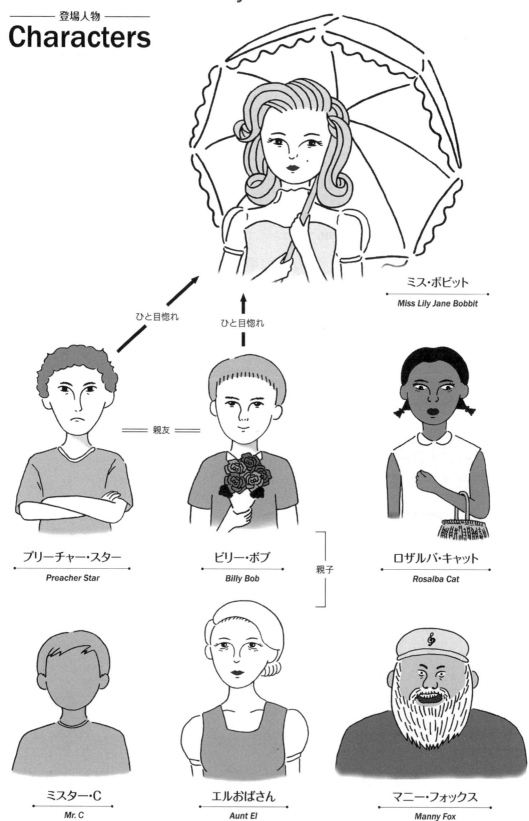

ミス・ボビット
Miss Lily Jane Bobbit

ひと目惚れ   ひと目惚れ

親友

親子

プリーチャー・スター
Preacher Star

ビリー・ボブ
Billy Bob

ロザルバ・キャット
Rosalba Cat

ミスター・C
Mr. C

エルおばさん
Aunt El

マニー・フォックス
Manny Fox

1940年代　アメリカ南部 ─────

ハリウッド女優を目指す都会的な少女ミス・ボビットがとある田舎町にやってきた。この町に住む2人の少年ビリー・ボブとプリー
チャー・スターはミス・ボビットにひと目惚れをする。2人は彼女の気を引こうとあらゆる行動に出るがまったく相手にされない。
ある日、この町にマニー・フォックスと名乗る男がやってきて、ハリウッド・スター発掘のコンテストが開催されることになった。
当然、ミス・ボビットも出場することになったが、そこから事件が起きる。

ミス・ボビット / *Miss Lily Jane Bobbit*

ハリウッド女優を目指す、都会的で大人びた少女。ある日、語り手たちが住む田舎町に引っ越してくる。レディの様に振
る舞い、最初は奇妙な目で見られるが、次第に街の人たちも彼女の振る舞いを受け入れていく。ロザルバとは姉妹にも
等しい関係。

ビリー・ボブ / *Billy Bob*

プリーチャーとは親友同士で常に一緒に行動している。突然やってきたミス・ボビットにひと目惚れをする。母親のエル
おばさんが丹精こめて栽培していた黄色いバラを勝手に摘みミス・ボビットにプレゼントしてしまう。ミス・ボビットの仕
事のアシスタントとして働くことになるが、これがきっかけでプリーチャーと仲違いをしてしまう。

プリーチャー・スター / *Preacher Star*

ガリガリに痩せた短髪の赤毛の少年。ビリーとは親友同士で常に一緒に行動している。突然やってきたミス・ボビットに
ひと目惚れをする。きつい癇癪持ちで町の人だけではなく身内からも恐れられている。

ロザルバ・キャット / *Rosalba Cat*

黒人の女の子。ビリーとプリーチャーにいじめられていたところを助けたミス・ボビットと姉妹関係を結び、常に行動を
共にする。

エルおばさん / *Aunt El*

ビリー・ボブの母。ビリーがバラを勝手に摘んだときはきつくお仕置きをしたりするが、息子に対して愛情深い母。

ミスター・C / *Mr. C*

この物語の語り手。ビリーの従兄弟でビリーの家に一緒に住んでいる。

マニー・フォックス / *Manny Fox*

詐欺師。ハリウッド・スター発掘オーディションを主催し、町の人たちから金を巻き上げた後に逃亡する。仕事の口利き
もしている。がっしりとした体格。

ミセス・ソーヤー / *Mrs. Sawyer*

ミス・ボビットの下宿先の女主人。雷を異常に恐れており、家の屋根には避雷針が20本以上ある。うわさ好き。

ミス・ボビットの母 / *Miss Lily Jane Bobbit's mother*

言葉が不自由でほとんど話さない。とても腕の良いお針子でコンテストで優勝したことがある。

Truman Capote

Children
on
Their
Birthdays

UNIT 1

---

the 1st paragraph

 **Warm Up**

Recite the following sentences out loud.

> 1. He went by the seven o'clock train.
> 2. I'm not sure if this is correct.
> 3. Something needs to be said about it.
> 4. Accidents will happen.
> 5. The roads were paved with asphalt.

Yesterday afternoon the six-o'clock bus ran over Miss Bobbit. I'm not sure what there is to be said about it; after all, she was only ten years old, still I know no one of us in this town will forget her. For one thing, nothing she ever did was ordinary, not from the first time that we saw her, and that was a year ago. Miss Bobbit and her mother, they arrived on that same six-o'clock bus, the one that comes through 5 from Mobile. It happened to be my cousin Billy Bob's birthday, and so most of the children in town were here at our house. We were sprawled on the front porch having tutti-frutti and devil cake when the bus stormed around Deadman's Curve. It was the summer that never rained; rusted dryness coated everything; sometimes when a car passed on the road, raised dust would hang in the still air an hour or more. Aunt El said 10 if they didn't pave the highway soon she was going to move down to the seacoast; but she'd said that for such a long time. Anyway, we were sitting on the porch, tutti-frutti melting on our plates, when suddenly, just as we were wishing that something would happen, something did; for out of the red road dust appeared Miss Bobbit. A wiry little girl in a starched, lemon-colored party dress, she sassed along with a grown-up 15 mince, one hand on her hip, the other supporting a spinsterish umbrella. Her mother, lugging two cardboard valises and a wind-up victrola, trailed in the background. She was a gaunt shaggy woman with silent eyes and a hungry smile.

NOTES

line

1 **Yesterday afternoon**「昨日の午後」この yesterday は afternoon の形容詞。yesterday morning「昨朝」、yesterday evening「昨晩」となるが、「昨夜」となると yesterday night より last night のほうが普通。

1 **bus**「バス」omnibus「乗合自動車」に由来する。英国では coach、米国では Greyhound などの長距離バスが発達しており、遠方の旅行にも利用される。

1 **ran over** > run over「(車などが) …をひく」

1 **Miss**「嬢」Miss は、年齢に関係なく、Lady または Dame の尊称で呼ばれない未婚女性の名の前につける一般的な敬称。最初、町の人々は 10 歳のボビットをばかにしてくすくす笑っている (snicker) が、やがて軽く会釈する (little bow) ようになる (第 11 段落参照)。

1 **Bobbit**「ボビット」本編の女性主人公 Miss Lily Jane Bobbit。作者 Capote の有名な『ティファニーで朝食を』(*Breakfast at Tiffany's*, 1958) のゴライトリー (Holiday (Holly) Golightly) と関連しており、両者の性格は、"unattached, unconventional wanderers, dreamers in pursuit of some ideal of happiness." と、カポーティの伯母 Marie Rudisill は述べている。

1 **what there is to be said about it** この is to > be to は「義務」を示す。

3 **For one thing**「一つには、まず一つ理由 (根拠) をあげるならば」多くの場合 for another が続いて理由などを説明する。

4 **not from the first time** = not ordinary from the first time …

6 **Mobile**「モービル」米国南東部の Alabama 州南部にある、メキシコ湾に臨む港湾都市で、千葉県市原市と姉妹都市。

7 **town**「(自分の住んでいる、あるいは今話題にしている) 町、都市」この意味は無冠詞で用いる。

8 **tutti-frutti**「トゥッティ・フルッティ (刻んだ果物の砂糖漬け入りアイスクリーム)」

8 **devil cake**「黒っぽい、(たいていの場合) チョコレートケーキ」

8 **stormed** > storm「(嵐のように) 突進する」

8 **Deadman's Curve**「デッドマンズ・カーブ」普通名詞 deadman's curve は、「(事故の多い) 魔のカーブ」

10 **still**「動きのない、静止した；風のない」still alive「まだ生きている」の副詞ではなく形容詞の意味。

10 **Aunt El**「エルおばさん」ボビット嬢に恋するビリー・ボブの母。El は、たとえば「エリノア」(Elenore)、他に Elena, Elen, Ellie などの愛称。語り手の「私」Mr. C から言うと叔母に当たる。

11 **pave**「(道路などを) 舗装する、(道路) に (砂利・煉瓦などを) 敷く」

14 **highway**「(市・町を結ぶ) 主要 (幹線) 道路、本街道」日本語の「ハイウエイ」は「高速道路」を意味するが、highway は「ハイウェイ」ではなく、「国道」「県道」などに相当する。英語で「高速道路」は、expressway, freeway, motorway, speedway, superhighway などとなる。

14 **for**「というのは〜」

14 **wiry**「(人・体などが) 引き締まった、(細身で) 筋肉質の」

15 **starched**「糊のきいた」starch は「(布など) にのりをつける、のりづけする」

15 **sassed** > sass「…に生意気を言う；…に口答えする (talk back)」

15 **grownup**「大人っぽい」反意語は childish。

16 **mince**「気取った話し方 (歩き方)」

16 **spinsterish**「未婚女性らしい」No longer in polite usage.

17 **lugging** > lug「(…を) 力まかせに引く；引きずる、無理に連れていく (drag)」

17 **cardboard**「ボール紙、厚紙 (カードや紙箱用)」

17 **valises** > valise「(米) 旅行用手さげかばん、スーツケース」発音注意 [[vlíːs; -z]]

17 **wind-up**「巻上げの；(おもちゃが) 手巻きぜんまいで動く」

17 **victrola**「蓄音機」Victrola「ヴィクトローラ」は、米国の Victor 社製の蓄音機の商品名。(昔の) 蝋管 (ろうかん) の旧式蓄音機で、ボビット嬢が踊りの練習のために使う。

17 **trailed** > trail「(疲れて) 足を引きずって歩く；だらだらと歩く」

18 **gaunt**「(病気などで) やつれて、やせこけた」

18 **shaggy**「(髪・毛など) もじゃもじゃの、くしゃくしゃの」

EXERCISES

Q1. Choose the most suitable word to each blank in the following summary from the word list blow.

The narrator says that yesterday afternoon the 6 p.m. bus (1) over ten-year-old Miss Bobbit. A year before, Miss Bobbit arrived on that very same (2) with her mother. It was the day of Billy Bob's (3) party. The children sat on the porch eating cake and ice cream. Miss Bobbit walked through the road (4) wearing a party dress, makeup, and carrying a parasol. She walked in a strangely adult manner while her mother dragged their (5) behind her.

[dust, ran, luggage, birthday, bus]

Q2. Mark the following sentences true (T) or false (F) according to the story. If it's false, correct it.

1. The narrator thinks everyone will remember Miss Bobbit because she was never ordinary. [　]
2. Miss Bobbit has been in town for ten years. [　]
3. The narrator is Billy Bob's cousin. [　]
4. Tutti-frutti is a kind of sandwich. [　]
5. The town is on the seacoast. [　]
6. The strangers who arrive in town are a chubby little girl and her fat, tired mother. [　]
7. The streets are dusty because they are unpaved, and it is a hot summer. [　]
8. Miss Bobbit's mother has a wind instrument. [　]

Q3. Match definition 1–8 with the appropriate word or phrase below.

1. lean and strong.   (   )

2. strong paper used for making boxes.   (   )

3. long, thick, and messy.   (   )

4. to spread in an untidy way; to cover a large area.   (   )

5. be cheeky or rude to somebody.   (   )

6. to move fast, to rush.   (   )

7. used to introduce one of two or more reasons.   (   )

8. to walk slowly because you are tired or bored, especially behind somebody else.

                                                                                (   )

[cardboard, for one thing, sass, shaggy, sprawl, storm, trail, wiry]

Q4. Choose the most suitable word or phrase from the list above to fill in the blanks. If necessary, correct the word form.

1. She burst into tears and (   ) off.

2. Bernadette was a small, (   ) woman.

3. The town (   ) along the side of the lake.

4. The mountain goat has a long, (   ) coat.

5. 'Why don't you get a car?' 'Well, (   ), I can't drive!'

6. The kids (   ) after us while we shopped for clothes.

7. Her mother warned her not to (   ) her teachers.

8. Most people try to recycle paper, (   ), plastic, and glass.

UNIT **2**

Warm Up
3

Recite the following sentences out loud.

> 1. His face grew pale.
> 2. The audience set up an awful clamor.
> 3. They fixed their attention on the sight.
> 4. The upper story is reached by stairs.
> 5. Suddenly he started laughing.

4

All the children on the porch had grown so still that when a cone of wasps started humming the girls did not set up their usual holler. Their attention was too fixed upon the approach of Miss Bobbit and her mother, who had by now reached the gate. "Begging your pardon," called Miss Bobbit in a voice that was at once silky and childlike, like a pretty piece of ribbon, and immaculately exact, like a movie star   5 or a schoolmarm, "but might we speak with the grown-up persons of the house?" This, of course, meant Aunt El; and, at least to some degree, myself. But Billy Bob and all the other boys, no one of whom was over thirteen, followed down to the gate after us. From their faces you would have thought they'd never seen a girl before. Certainly not like Miss Bobbit. As Aunt El said, whoever heard tell of a child wearing   10 makeup? Tangee gave her lips an orange glow, her hair, rather like a costume wig, was a mass of rosy curls, and her eyes had a knowing, penciled tilt; even so, she had a skinny dignity, she was a lady, and, what is more, she looked you in the eye with manlike directness. "I'm Miss Lily Jane Bobbit, Miss Bobbit from Memphis, Tennessee," she said solemnly. The boys looked down at their toes, and, on the porch,   15 Cora McCall, who Billy Bob was courting at the time, led the girls into a fanfare of giggles. "*Country* children," said Miss Bobbit with an understanding smile, and gave her parasol a saucy whirl. "My mother," and this homely woman allowed an abrupt nod to acknowledge herself, "my mother and I have taken rooms here. Would you be so kind as to point out the house? It belongs to a Mrs. Sawyer." Why, sure, said Aunt   20

NOTES

line

1 **grown** > grow「（補語を伴って）（次第に）…になる、なっていく (become, turn)」

1 **still**（形）「静止した、じっとした」

1 **a cone of wasps**「円錐形状のスズメバチの群れ」cone /kóʊn/ であって、corn /kɔ́ɚn | kɔ́ːn/「とうもろこし」ではない。

2 **set up**「（騒ぎ）を起こす、（大声）を上げる」

2 **holler**「叫び、大声、わめき」同義語 shout, scream, shriek, screech, squeal, yell etc.

4 **Begging your pardon** > I beg your pardon「失礼ですが」見知らぬ人に話しかける時、また他人と意見を異にした場合に自説を述べる時のていねいな言葉であるのは周知の通り。

4 **at once**「（and と相関的に用いて）…でも（また…でも）(both)」

4 **silky**「（態度・声などが）もの柔らかな、当たりの穏やかな」

5 **immaculately** > immaculate「欠点のない、完全な (perfect)」

6 **schoolmarm**「（衒学的で堅苦しいタイプの）先生くさい人（女にも男にも用いる）」marm = ma'am「（女性に対する丁寧な呼び掛けとして）（米）奥様、奥さん；先生」

7 **Aunt El**「エルおばさん」Unit 1、10 行目の注参照。

7 **Certainly not like Miss Bobbit.** → Certainly (they had) not (seen a girl) like Miss Bobbit (before).

10 **whoever heard tell of a child wearing makeup?** → whoever heard anyone tell of a child wearing makeup?

11 **Tangee**「タンジー社の口紅」tangerine（濃い橙色、赤橙色）を特色とした色合いの Tangee lipstick が 1940 年代には全米 1 位の売れ行きとなった。創業は George William Luft (1869–1939)

11 **costume**（形）「特定の衣装にふさわしい（の効果を高める）」

11 **wig**「かつら（舞台用・女性のおしゃれ用など）」男性のはげ隠し用では toupee（発音注意 /tuːpéɪ/）という言い方もある。17–18 世紀ヨーロッパで流行し、現在でも英国では裁判官や弁護士が法廷でつける。

12 **knowing**「抜け目のない；心得顔の」

12 **penciled**「上品に書かれた、優美に彩色された」

12 **tilt** = eyeliner. ふつうは、a position in which one end or side of something is higher than the other; an act of tilting something to one side のような意味。

13 **dignity**「威厳、重々しさ、品位」a person of dignity 気品のある人。

13 **lady**「身分の高い気品のある女性、貴婦人；教養があり優雅で気品のある女性、淑女、レディー」用例としては、She is not quite a lady. とても淑女などではない、She is a real lady. ほんとうの淑女だ、She is a lady by birth. 生まれは良家の女性だ、など。

14 **directness**「率直さ」

14 **Memphis, Tennessee**「テネシー州メンフィス」米国 Tennessee 州南西部 Mississippi 河畔最大の港市・鉄道網の中心となる工業都市。

15 **solemnly**「厳かに、厳粛に、荘重に」

16 **court**「（人の）支持（歓心）を得ようとする、機嫌を取る、（人に）取り入る、こびる」

16 **fanfare**「ファンファーレ」発音注意 /fǽnfeɚ/。

17 **giggle**「（通例、愚かしく、とくに女の子が）クスクス（クックッ、フフフ、イヒヒ、キャッキャッ、ヒャッヒャッ）と笑う」

18 **parasol**「パラソル、（女性用）日傘」語源は、para「防護」+ sol「太陽」から。「ビーチパラソル」は和製英語で、英語では beach umbrella となる。

18 **saucy**「（人・言葉・ふるまいなど）生意気な、ずうずうしい」

18 **whirl**「回転」

18 **homely**「容姿が人並み以下の、器量の悪い」

20 **a**「（固有名詞につけて）…とかいう人 (one)」

20 **Why**「（意外なことの発見・承認などの際の発声として）あら！、おや！、まあ！；もちろんさ！、そりゃ！」疑問詞ではなく間投詞。

El, that's Mrs. Sawyer's, right there across the street. The only boarding house around here, it is an old tall dark place with about two dozen lightning rods scattered on the roof: Mrs. Sawyer is scared to death in a thunderstorm.

Coloring like an apple, Billy Bob said, please ma'am, it being such a hot day and all, wouldn't they rest a spell and have some tutti-frutti? and Aunt El said yes, by all 25 means, but Miss Bobbit shook her head. "Very fattening, tutti-frutti; but *merci* you kindly," and they started across the road, the mother half-dragging her parcels in the dust. Then, and with an earnest expression, Miss Bobbit turned back; the sunflower yellow of her eyes darkened, and she rolled them slightly sideways, as if trying to remember a poem. "My mother has a disorder of the tongue, so it is necessary that I 30 speak for her," she announced rapidly and heaved a sigh. "My mother is a very fine seamstress; she has made dresses for the society of many cities and towns, including Memphis and Tallahassee. No doubt you have noticed and admired the dress I am wearing. Every stitch of it was hand-sewn by my mother. My mother can copy any pattern, and just recently she won a twenty-five-dollar prize from the *Ladies' Home* 35 *Journal*. My mother can also crochet, knit and embroider. If you want any kind of sewing done, please come to my mother. Please advise your friends and family. Thank you." And then, with a rustle and a swish, she was gone.

21 **boarding house**「賄い付き下宿屋，食事付き民宿；寄宿舎」普通 rooming ((UK) lodging) house（賄いなし）より上等。

22 **lightning rods** > lightning rod「避雷針」lightning「稲妻」

24 **Coloring** > color「色が変わる；（人が）顔を赤くする (≒ blush) (up; at)」

25 **spell**「しばらくの間 (a little while)」a spell ago [back]（米）しばらく前。

26 **merci**「ありがとう (thank you)」

28 **sunflower**「ひまわり」米国 Kansas 州の州花。

29 **darkened** > darken「陰鬱（いんうつ）（陰気）になる；（表情が）けわしくなる」

31 **heaved a sigh** [groan] > heave a sigh「ため息をつく，うめき声をあげる」

33 **Tallahassee**「タラハシー」米国 Florida 州北部の都市で同州の州都。

35 **twenty-five-dollar**「（おそらく現在の）1 万円（程度）」執筆当時 1940 年代（第二次世界大戦が 1939–1945 年）の円相場は、1940 年の $1 ≒ ¥4.2 から 1949 年の $1 ≒ ¥360 まで大きく変動する。

35 *Ladies' Home Journal*「レディズ・ホーム・ジャーナル（婦人家庭誌）」1883 年 Meredith Corporation が創刊し、まもなく 40 万部の発行部数を実現して企業としての大衆出版の記録をつくり、1903 年には 100 万人の購読者を獲得し、全米第一の雑誌となる。

36 **crochet**「クローシェ編み（かぎ針編み）をする」

36 **embroider**「刺繍する」

37 **rustle**「さらさら、かさかさいう音；衣ずれの音」

38 **swish**「衣ずれの音；（杖・むちの）ヒューヒューいう音；（水などの）シューという音」

"a Mrs. Sawyer" (p. 6, l. 22)

この場合の a は、固有名詞につけて「…という人」の意味になります。例えば、a Mr. Smith「スミスさんという人」です。

one で処理する場合もあります。one (Mr.) Smith「スミスさんという人」。しかし、a Mr. (Dr, etc.) Smith の形のほうが普通ですし certain が付く場合もあります。a certain Mr. Smith「スミスさんとかいう人」。

A Mr. Hill has come to see you.「ヒルさんという方がお見えです」

他にも類似した例としては、a happy Bush「うれしそうなブッシュ氏」、a Stuart「スチュアート家の人」、a Picasso「ピカソの作品」、a Newton「ニュートンのような人（大科学者）」などがあります。文で言うと、He's bought a Honda (Ford).「彼はホンダ（フォード）の車を買った」とか、Is that painting a Rembrandt?「あの絵画はレンブラントですか」

他に and の用法とも関連しますが、a poet and novelist と a poet and a novelist は異なります。前者は、「詩人にして小説家 1 人」であるのに、後者は、通例「詩人と小説家 2 人」の意味です。ただし、He was an actor and a playwright. と言った場合、1 人で 2 面の活動または性質を強調するときは両方に冠詞がつき、意味は「彼は俳優でありかつ劇作家であった」となり、結局 1 人のことで、彼が 2 人であるわけはありません。二刀流 two-way star の大谷翔平選手は、各紙で (both) a hitter and a pitcher と紹介されています。

他のモノの用例では、A carriage and four was passing by.「四頭立ての馬車が通り過ぎていった」、a cup and saucer「（セットになった）茶わんと受け皿、a watch and chain「鎖つきの時計」という意味になります。

EXERCISES

Q1. Choose the most suitable word to each blank in the following summary from the word list blow.

The boys stare at the pretty girl approaching the house. Miss Bobbit asks if she can speak with the "(1) persons of the house." She introduces herself to Aunt El as Miss Lily Jane Bobbit, telling her they have come from Memphis, Tennessee. She asks for (2) to the boarding house where she and her mother have taken rooms. Billy Bob invites Miss Bobbit to stay and have ice cream, but she refuses because ice cream is (3). Miss Bobbit tells everyone that her mother cannot (4). Also, she says that her mother is an excellent (5) who made the dress Miss Bobbit is certain they have all been admiring.

[directions, fattening, speak, seamstress, grown-up]

Q2. Mark the following sentences true (T) or false (F) according to the story. If it's false, correct it.

1. The girls on the porch are usually calm when troubled by wasps. [   ]
2. A "pretty piece of ribbon" is sewn to Miss Bobbit's dress. [   ]
3. Miss Bobbit is charmed by the polite manners of the country children. [   ]
4. Miss Bobbit and her mother are renting a room in a house across the street from the narrator's house. [   ]
5. Billy Bob uses crayons to fill in apples in a coloring book. [   ]
6. Miss Bobbit says her mother has trouble speaking. [   ]
7. Miss Bobbit buys her dresses in Memphis and Tallahassee. [   ]
8. Miss Bobbit's mother won twenty-five dollars for her sewing skill. [   ]

Q3. Match definition 1–8 with the appropriate word or phrase below.

1. a short period of time.   (   )
2. simultaneously.   (   )
3. sudden and unexpected.   (   )
4. a calm and serious manner that deserves respect.   (   )
5. free from flaws or mistakes; perfect.   (   )
6. unattractive in appearance.   (   )
7. bold and lively.   (   )
8. an audible exhalation expressing sadness, relief, or tiredness. (   )

[at once, abrupt, dignity, homely, immaculate, saucy, sigh, spell]

Q4. Choose the most suitable word or phrase from the list above to fill in the blanks. If necessary, correct the word form.

1. She let out a long (   ) of despair.
2. I was surprised by the (   ) change of subject.
3. He was popular even though he was (   ).
4. In the low light of the gallery the effect is (   ) beautiful and rather ominous.
5. She accepted the criticism with quiet (   ).
6. His early career was interrupted by various short (   ) in prison for violent behavior.
7. Her wardrobe for the fall-spring season also changed and she adopted a bold, (   ) and fashion-forward style.
8. A doctor who had an (   ) professional record avoided police arrest.

UNIT **3**

Warm Up

Recite the following sentences out loud.

> 1. He said he had not discussed the matter with her. Furthermore, he had not even contacted her.
> 2. All his dreams came true.
> 3. You ought not to act like that in public space.
> 4. Before she left the room, she closed the window.
> 5. The students straightened up when they heard the whistle.

Cora McCall and the girls pulled their hair-ribbons nervously, suspiciously, and looked very put out and prune-faced. I'm *Miss* Bobbit, said Cora, twisting her face into an evil imitation, and I'm Princess Elizabeth, that's who I am, ha, ha, ha. Furthermore, said Cora, that dress was just as tacky as could be; personally, Cora said, all my clothes come from Atlanta; plus a pair of shoes from New York, which is 5
not even to mention my silver turquoise ring all the way from Mexico City, Mexico. Aunt El said they ought not to behave that way about a fellow child, a stranger in the town, but the girls went on like a huddle of witches, and certain boys, the sillier ones that liked to be with the girls, joined in and said things that made Aunt El go red and declare she was going to send them all home and tell their daddies, to boot. But 10
before she could carry forward this threat Miss Bobbit herself intervened by traipsing across the Sawyer porch, costumed in a new and startling manner.

The older boys, like Billy Bob and Preacher Star, who had sat quiet while the girls razzed Miss Bobbit, and who had watched the house into which she'd disappeared with misty, ambitious faces, they now straightened up and ambled down to the gate. 15
Cora McCall sniffed and poked out her lower lip, but the rest of us went and sat on the steps. Miss Bobbit paid us no mind whatever. The Sawyer yard is dark with mulberry trees and it is planted with grass and sweet shrub. Sometimes after a rain you can smell the sweet shrub all the way into our house; and in the center of this yard there

NOTES

2 **put out**「（俗語）怒った、不機嫌な」

2 **prune-faced**「（干しすもものように）顔をしかめて、不賛成の様子で」

2 **I'm *Miss* Bobbit,** Cora が Miss Bobbit の言ったことをまねて言っている。引用符 (quotation mark) が付いていないので注意。また、イタリック（斜字）はこの言葉を強調して言っていることを示す。

4 **tacky**「やぼったい、時代遅れの」

5 **Atlanta**「アトランタ」アメリカ南部ジョージア州の州都。南部の大都市のひとつ。

6 **silver turquoise ring**「ターコイズをあしらった銀の指輪」

6 **Mexico City**「メキシコ・シティ」メキシコの首都。

7 **fellow** 名詞で「仲間」。ここでは形容詞、「仲間の、同じ身分の」。

8 **sillier** > silly（形）「ばかな、単純な」の比較級。

10 **boot**（動）「（強く）蹴る、蹴とばす」

11 **Miss Bobbit herself**「ミス・ボビット自身が」人・人名の後に ~self が続く場合、「〜自身」という強調の表現。

11 **intervened** > intervene [ìntəví:n]（動）「間に入る、割り込む」

11 **traipsing** > traipse（動）「（話・方言）ぶらつく、うろうろ歩く」

12 **the Sawyer porch**「ソーヤー夫人の家のポーチ」porch は南部の家でよく見られる張り出し玄関。

14 **razzed** > razz「あざける、からかって笑う」

15 **misty**「ぼやけた、はっきりしない」mist（名）「霧」から派生して、「あいまいな、なにかを含んだような」。

15 **ambled down to** > amble down to「〜へ向かってゆったり歩いていく」

16 **sniffed** > sniff「鼻を鳴らす」この場面では不快な気持を表す。

16 **poked out** > poke out「ぐっと突き出す」

17 **paid us no mind whatever**「僕らにはまったく注意を向けなかった」whatever が否定文で使われる場合は「少しの〜も」の意。

18 **mulberry trees**「クワの木」赤や黒紫色の実がなる。

18 **sweet shrub**「クロバナロウバイ」頑丈な低木で、甘い香りのする暗褐色の花をつける。

19 **you can smell** この you は特定の人物を指すのではなく、「（一般的に）〜だ」の意。

is a sundial which Mrs. Sawyer installed in 1912 as a memorial to her Boston bull, 20
Sunny, who died after having lapped up a bucket of paint. Miss Bobbit pranced into
the yard toting the victrola, which she put on the sundial; she wound it up, and started
a record playing, and it played "The Count of Luxembourg." By now it was almost
nightfall, a firefly hour, blue as milkglass; and birds like arrows swooped together and
swept into the folds of trees. Before storms, leaves and flowers appear to burn with 25
a private light, color, and Miss Bobbit, got up in a little white skirt like a powderpuff
and with strips of gold-glittering tinsel ribboning her hair, seemed, set against the
darkening all around, to contain this illuminated quality. She held her arms arched
over her head, her hands lily-limp, and stood straight up on the tips of her toes. She
stood that way for a good long while, and Aunt El said it was right smart of her. Then 30
she began to waltz around and around, and around and around she went until Aunt
El said, why, she was plain dizzy from the sight. She stopped only when it was time
to rewind the victrola; and when the moon came rolling down the ridge, and the last
supper bell had sounded, and all the children had gone home, and the night iris was
beginning to bloom, Miss Bobbit was still there in the dark turning like a top. 35

20 **sundial**「日時計」目盛版の上に指針を立て、太陽の日周運動で変化する指針の影の指す目盛を読み時刻を測る。

20 **Boston bull, Sunny**　ソーヤー夫人が飼っていたボストン・テリアのサニー。

21 **lapped up** > lap up「（犬などが）ぺろぺろとなめる、飲む」

21 **pranced** > prance「はねながら進む、意気揚々と進む」

22 **toting** > tote [tout]「運ぶ」

23 **"The Count of Luxembourg"**『ルクセンブルク伯爵』1909 年にウィーンで初演されたオペレッタ。若き放蕩貴族ルネ・ルクセンブルク伯爵を軸とした恋愛もの。最後は 3 組の婚姻が成立し大団円を迎える。

23 **by now**「そのころまでには」

24 **a firefly hour**「ほたるが飛び始める時間」

24 **blue as milkglass**「ミルクグラスの様に青い」milkglass は花瓶などに使われる不透明なガラスで、白のほかに青やピンクなど様々な色がある。

24 **birds like arrows swooped together**「鳥たちが矢のようにさっと舞い降りた」like arrows は挿入句。swoop がこの部分の動詞。

25 **with a private light, color,**「それだけが持つような光や色」の意。private には「特定の誰か、なにかだけに属する」という意味がある。

27 **strips of gold-glittering tinsel**「金色に光るティンセルのひも」glittering は動詞 glitter「きらきら光る」から派生した形容詞、「輝く、きらびやかな」。ティンセルは金糸などを織り込んでいて、安っぽい装飾などに使われる。

28 **to contain this illuminated quality**「この輝く性質を内に持っている」ただし、この輝きが tinsel であることにも注意。

29 **her hands lily-limp**　(hold) her hands lily-limp「手をユリの様に弱々しく上げて」

30 **it was right smart of her**「こんなことをするとはあの子は賢い娘だね」right は副詞、「まさしく、非常に」。

32 **why**　間投詞「あら、おや」。疑問詞の「なぜ」ではないので注意。

32 **plain dizzy**　plain はここでは副詞、「はっきりと、すっかり」。dizzy（形）「めまいでふらふらする、目が回る」。

32 **She stopped only when ~**「彼女が止まったのは~する時だけだった」

33 **rewind** [riːˈwaɪnd]「巻き直す」

33 **when the moon came rolling down the ridge**「月が山の尾根を落ちてきた時」月が沈む様子を表現している。ridge は「山の背、尾根」。

34 **supper bell**　夕食の時間を知らせるベル。

34 **night iris**　アイリスは昼に咲く種と夜に咲く種がある。また、アイリスは死者の魂を天国に連れて行くとされた。テネシー州の州花でもある。

35 **top**「（名）こま」

EXERCISES

Q1. Choose the most suitable word to each blank in the following summary from the word list blow.

The girls and some of the boys (1) at Miss Bobbit after she leaves, ridiculing her manners and odd ways. Aunt El becomes (2) at the children for gossiping rudely about the newcomers. The older boys (3) the other girls on the porch. They are (4) to the new girl in town and eager to see more of her. Across the street at the boarding house, Miss Bobbit comes out to the yard, plays music on the victrola and (5). The boys watch, fascinated. Miss Bobbit continues to dance in the dark after the children go home.

[angry, dances, attracted, laugh, ignore]

Q2. Mark the following sentences true (T) or false (F) according to the story. If it's false, correct it.

1. Cora McCall and her friends loudly admire Miss Bobbit and her dress.   [   ]
2. Cora vacations in Atlanta, New York and Mexico City.   [   ]
3. The narrator compares the girls to witches because they gossip viciously. [   ]
4. Aunt El scolds the children for ridiculing strangers.   [   ]
5. Billy Bob and Preacher Star walk down to the front gate so they can escape the party quickly.   [   ]
6. Miss Bobbit waves to the children before she begins to dance.   [   ]
7. "The Count of Luxemborg" is a piece of music.   [   ]
8. Miss Bobbit stops dancing as soon as the children leave the party.   [   ]

Q3. Match definition 1–8 with the appropriate word or phrase below.

1. shining brightly or sparkling.   (   )
2. to do things in a way that people think is correct or polite.   (   )
3. a children's toy that spins.   (   )
4. to make a film or recording go back to an earlier point.   (   )
5. acting in a way that inspires distrust.   (   )
6. to delay or prevent something from happening.   (   )
7. determined to be successful.   (   )
8. an unknown person, a visitor.   (   )

[**ambitious, behave, glittering, intervene,
rewind, stranger, suspiciously, top**]

**Q4. Choose the most suitable word or phrase from the list above to fill in the
blanks. If necessary, correct the word form.**

1. It's always exciting when a (   ) comes to town.
2. She has a (   ) diamond necklace.
3. My boss (   ) and shut down the investigation.
4. He used to (   ) like a true gentleman.
5. The children have a wooden (   ) that they spin on the floor.
6. My sister is an (   ) person, and she founded her own company last year.
7. The man kept looking at us (   ) as we were in funny costumes.
8. Can you (   ) the tape so that we can watch that scene again?

UNIT **4**

the 6th and 7th paragraphs

 Warm Up
9

Recite the following sentences out loud.

> 1. We did not see him again as he left the town for good.
> 2. She is afraid of spiders.
> 3. Last Easter they had a big party.
> 4. I used to play chess when I was young.
> 5. The children stand around chatting during their break.

We did not see her again for some time. Preacher Star came every morning to our house and stayed straight through to supper. Preacher is a rail-thin boy with a butchy shock of red hair; he has eleven brothers and sisters, and even they are afraid of him, for he has a terrible temper, and is famous in these parts for his green-eyed meanness: last fourth of July he whipped Ollie Overton so bad that Ollie's family had to send ⁵ him to the hospital in Pensacola; and there was another time he bit off half a mule's ear, chewed it and spit it on the ground. Before Billy Bob got his growth, Preacher played the devil with him, too. He used to drop cockleburrs down his collar, and rub pepper in his eyes, and tear up his homework. But now they are the biggest friends in town: talk alike, walk alike; and occasionally they disappear together for whole days, ¹⁰ Lord knows where to. But during these days when Miss Bobbit did not appear they stayed close to the house. They would stand around in the yard trying to slingshot sparrows off telephone poles; or sometimes Billy Bob would play his ukulele, and they would sing so loud Uncle Billy Bob, who is Judge for this county, claimed he could hear them all the way to the courthouse: *send me a letter*, *send it by mail*, *send* ¹⁵ *it in care of the Birmingham jail*. Miss Bobbit did not hear them; at least she never poked her head out the door. Then one day Mrs. Sawyer, coming over to borrow a cup of sugar, rattled on a good deal about her new boarders. You know, she said, squinting her chicken-bright eyes, the husband was a crook, uh huh, the child told me herself. Hasn't an ounce of shame, not a mite. Said her daddy was the dearest daddy and the ²⁰

NOTES

line

2 **rail-thin**「針金みたいに細い」

2 **butchy**「短い角刈りの」

3 **shock**（名）「もじゃもじゃの髪」

4 **his green-eyed meanness**「物事をひがんで見る意地の悪さ」green-eyed は嫉妬ぶかさや妬みを表すとされた。シェイクスピアの『オセロー』(*Othello*) では嫉妬のことを「緑の目をした怪物 (green-ey'd monster)」と表現している。

5 **last fourth of July**「去年の 7 月 4 日」7 月 4 日はアメリカの独立記念日で、もっとも重要な祝日の一つ。様々なイベントが各地で行われ、人々は家族や友人で過ごしたり旅行に出かけたりする。

6 **Pensacola**「ペンサコラ」フロリダ州北西部の港市。

7 **Before Billy Bob got his growth** = Before Billy Bob grew

8 **played the devil with him**「彼に対してひどいことをした」

8 **cockleburrs** > cocklebur「オナモミ」とげのある雑草。

11 **Lord knows where to**「どこへ行ったかは神のみぞ知る」

12 **slingshot**「ゴム銃で撃つ」

13 **telephone poles**「(電話線の) 電柱」

13 **ukulele**「ウクレレ」ギターに似た小さな四弦楽器。

14 **so loud**　このあとの that が省略されている。「とても大きな声でうたったので、〜」。

14 **Judge**（名）「判事」町に一人だけの場合、大文字で表す。

15 **courthouse**「裁判所の庁舎」court はそもそも四角い空間を指す。裁判所、宮廷、テニスコートなども court.

18 **rattled on** > rattle on「ぺちゃくちゃとしゃべる」

18 **boarder**（名）「下宿人」boarding house は下宿屋。

18 **squinting her chicken-bright eyes**「鶏みたいに光る眼を細めて」squint (動) は「目を細める、横目で見る」。

19 **crook**「詐欺師、盗人」

20 **Hasn't an ounce of shame, not a mite.**　主語の she が省略されている。次の文も同様。an ounce of 〜は「1 オンスの、ほんの少しの」、not a mite は「ダニほども、これっぽっちも」。

sweetest singing man in the whole of Tennessee . . . . And I said, honey, where is he? and just as off-hand as you please she says, Oh, he's in the penitentiary and we don't hear from him no more. Say, now, does that make your blood run cold? Uh huh, and I been thinking, her mama, I been thinking she's some kind a foreigner: never says a word, and sometimes it looks like she don't understand what nobody says to her. And you know, they eat everything *raw*. *Raw* eggs, *raw* turnips, carrots—no meat whatsoever. For reasons of health, the child says, but ho! she's been straight out on the bed running a fever since last Tuesday.

That same afternoon Aunt El went out to water her roses, only to discover them gone. These were special roses, ones she'd planned to send to the flower show in Mobile, and so naturally she got a little hysterical. She rang up the Sheriff, and said, listen here, Sheriff, you-come over here right fast. I mean somebody's got off with all my Lady Anne's that I've devoted myself to heart and soul since early spring. When the Sheriff's car pulled up outside our house, all the neighbors along the street came out on their porches, and Mrs. Sawyer, layers of cold cream whitening her face, trotted across the road. Oh shoot, she said, very disappointed to find no one had been murdered, oh shoot, she said, nobody's stole them roses. Your Billy Bob brought them roses over and left them for little Bobbit. Aunt El did not say one word. She just marched over to the peach tree, and cut herself a switch. Ohhh, Billy Bob, she stalked along the street calling his name, and then she found him down at Speedy's garage where he and Preacher were watching Speedy take a motor apart. She simply lifted him by the hair and, switching blueblazes, towed him home. But she couldn't make him say he was sorry and she couldn't make him cry. And when she was finished with him he ran into the backyard and climbed high into the tower of a pecan tree and swore he wasn't ever going to come down. Then his daddy came home, and it was time to have supper. His daddy stood at the window and called to him: Son, we aren't mad with you, so come down and eat your supper. But Billy Bob wouldn't budge. Aunt El went and leaned against the tree. She spoke in a voice soft as the gathering light. I'm sorry, son, she said, I didn't mean whipping you so hard like that. I've fixed a nice supper, son, potato salad and boiled ham and deviled eggs. Go away, said Billy Bob, I don't want no supper, and I hate you like all-fire. His daddy said he ought not to talk like that to his mother, and she began to cry. She stood there under the tree and cried, raising the hem of her skirt to dab at her eyes. I don't hate you, son . . . . If I didn't love you I wouldn't whip you. The pecan leaves began to rattle; Billy Bob slid slowly to the ground, and Aunt El, rushing her fingers through his hair, pulled him against her. Aw, Ma, he said, Aw, Ma.

22 **just as offhand as you please** 「まったくなにも気にしないで」offhand は「ぶっきらぼうに、即座に」、as ~ as you please は「好きなだけ~、どれだけでも」といった意味。

22 **penitentiary** 「刑務所」penitence はキリスト教の悔い改め、ざんげ。

23 **make your blood run cold** make A B「A を B にする」、使役用法。your blood が A, run cold が B に当たる。

24 **I been thinking** 正しくは I have been thinking ~.

24 **never says a word** 主語の she が省略されている。

25 **she don't understand what nobody says to her** = she doesn't understand what anybody says to her.

26 **no meat whatsoever** no ~ whatsoever は強調表現で「どんな~もない、しない」。

27 **straight out** 「ずっと~」

28 **running a fever** run には「(望ましくない状態に)なる」の意味がある。

29 **to water her roses** この water は動詞で「水をやる」。

29 **only to discover them gone** only to ~「…の結果、ただ~しただけだった」

30 **ones she'd planned to send** ones は roses のこと。she'd 以降は roses を修飾。

31 **got a little hysterical** get + 形容詞「(形容詞)になる」。

31 **the Sheriff** 「保安官」小さな町では通常保安官は一人だけなので、the + 大文字で表す。

32 **got off with** > get off with~「~を持って立ち去る」

33 **Lady Anne's** 「レディ・アン」バラの品種名。

35 **layers of cold cream whitening her face** 挿入句で、Mrs. Sawyer を修飾。「顔をまっ白にするほどコールドクリームをぶあつく塗って」。

36 **Oh shoot** shoot は間投詞、「ちぇっ」の意味。

36 **very disappointed ~** she (Mrs. Sawyer) に接続し、付帯状況を表す。

37 **nobody's stole them roses** = nobody's stolen those roses.

39 **cut herself a switch** 「自分が使うために小枝を折った」

39 **stalked along the street** 「(Billy Bobb を)求めて通りを歩いていった」stalk は「(獲物を求めて~を)歩き回る」の意味がある。

40 **Speedy's garage** 「スピーディーのガレージ」Speedy は人名、おそらく町の自動車修理工。

41 **watching Speedy take a motor apart** watch A 動詞で「A が~するのを見る」。take ~ apart で「~を分解する」。

41 **lifted him by the hair** 「髪をつかんで彼を引っ張り上げた」

42 **switching blueblazes** switching は動詞 switch「むちを振る」の分詞構文、「むちを振りながら」。blueblazes は俗語、「ひどく、めちゃくちゃに」。

43 **when she was finished with him** この部分の finish は「(おしおきが)終わる」の意味。

44 **pecan tree** 「ペカンの木」アメリカ南部、クルミ科の高木。実がなり、ピーカンナッツとも呼ばれる。

47 **mad with ~** 「~に腹を立てて、怒って」

47 **wouldn't budge** この wouldn't は強い拒絶、「どうしても~しようとしない」。budge「意見を変える、譲歩する」。

48 **the gathering light** 「光の集まり、日だまり」

49 **fixed a nice supper** fix はアメリカ俗語で「~を整える、用意する」の意味がある。

50 **deviled egg** 「デビルドエッグ」かたゆで卵を半分に切り、黄身をマヨネーズやドレッシングなどであえて白身に詰め直した料理。

51 **I hate you like all-fire** 「母さんなんか大嫌いだ」like は「~のように、まるで」、all-fire は俗語で「ひどく、ものすごく」。

53 **If I didn't love you I wouldn't whip you.** 仮定法過去 If I (過去形) ~ I would ….「もし~なら、…だろう」。

55 **rushing her fingers through his hair** 分詞構文の副詞節が挿入句として使われている。「彼の髪を指で強くすきながら」。

56 **Aw, Ma,** 「ああ、母さん」

Q1. Choose the most suitable word to each blank in the following summary from the word list blow.

After that first day, no one (1) Miss Bobbit for some time. The boys hang around the boarding house, singing and performing, trying to get Miss Bobbit's (2). Mrs. Sawyer, the owner of the boarding house, tells Aunt El that Miss Bobbit's father is in (3). Mrs. Sawyer also comments on the odd ways of the mother and daughter, such as eating all their food raw. Aunt El discovers all her (4) have been taken and calls the Sheriff. Mrs. Sawyer tells Aunt El that her roses weren't stolen. Billy Bob gave them to Miss Bobbit. Aunt El punishes Billy Bob, but he refuses to (5). Later, Aunt El apologizes to her son for losing her temper.

[**apologize, jail, roses, sees, attention**]

Q2. Mark the following sentences true (T) or false (F) according to the story. If it's false, correct it.

1. Preacher Star is famous for having eleven brothers and sisters. [   ]
2. Ollie Overton was beaten so badly by Preacher that he had to go to the hospital.

   [   ]
3. Preacher Star and Billy Bob stay in front of Billy Bob's house and sing too loud because they are afraid of running into the two strangers. [   ]
4. Mrs. Sawyer spreads gossip about Miss Bobbit and her mother. [   ]
5. When the roses disappear, Aunt El goes to bed with a fever. [   ]
6. Mrs. Sawyer tells Aunt El that Billy Bob gave her roses to Miss Bobbit. [   ]
7. Aunt El whips Billy Bob for stealing the roses. [   ]
8. After being whipped, Billy Bob cries and apologizes. [   ]

Q3. Match definition 1–8 with the appropriate word or phrase below.

1. to take something from another and return it later.　　　(　　　　)

2. the edge of cloth that is turned down and sewn, such as on a skirt or dress.

　　　　　　　　　　　　　　　　　　　　　　　　(　　　　)

3. an officer responsible for keeping law and order in a county or town.

　　　　　　　　　　　　　　　　　　　　　　　　(　　　　)

4. not standing straight, resting weight on something.　　　(　　　　)

5. a casual or disinterested manner.　　　　　　　　　　(　　　　)

6. the authority in a court, the one who decides how criminals are punished.

　　　　　　　　　　　　　　　　　　　　　　　　(　　　　)

7. to give time or attention to something.　　　　　　　　(　　　　)

8. the last meal of the day, less formal than dinner.　　　　(　　　　)

[borrow, devote to, hem, Judge, lean, off-hand, Sheriff, supper]

Q4. Choose the most suitable word or phrase from the list above to fill in the blanks. If necessary, correct the word form.

1. The (　　　　　) of our town is committed to the safety of the town.

2. She was tired and (　　　　　) against the wall to rest.

3. Can I (　　　　　) your umbrella?

4. The amount of time (　　　　　) leisure is dropping.

5. She held up the (　　　　　) of her dress to avoid getting mud on it.

6. The (　　　　　) ruled that the evidence could not be used.

7. I'll do my homework after (　　　　　).

8. The president talked in an (　　　　　) everyday way.

UNIT 5

•••

the 8th, 9th and 10th paragraphs

 Warm Up

Recite the following sentences out loud.

> 1. I felt sorry for her because she was at a loss.
> 2. An empty boat was drifting on the lake.
> 3. We couldn't tell by his looks if he was happy or not.
> 4. He tried to continue as though nothing had happened.
> 5. The kitty was the sweetest thing he ever saw in his life.

After supper Billy Bob came and flung himself on the foot of my bed. He smelled
all sour and sweet, the way boys do, and I felt very sorry for him, especially because
he looked so worried. His eyes were almost shut with worry. You're s'posed to send
sick folks flowers, he said righteously. About this time we heard the victrola, a lilting
faraway sound, and a night moth flew through the window, drifting in the air delicate   5
as the music. But it was dark now, and we couldn't tell if Miss Bobbit was dancing.
Billy Bob, as though he were in pain, doubled up on the bed like a jackknife; but his
face was suddenly clear, his grubby boy-eyes twitching like candles. She's so cute,
he whispered, she's the cutest dickens I ever saw, gee, to hell with it, I don't care, I'd
pick all the roses in China.   10

Preacher would have picked all the roses in China, too. He was as crazy about
her as Billy Bob. But Miss Bobbit did not notice them. The sole communication we
had with her was a note to Aunt El thanking her for the flowers. Day after day she
sat on her porch, always dressed to beat the band, and doing a piece of embroidery,
or combing curls in her hair, or reading a Webster's dictionary—formal, but friendly   15
enough; if you said good-day to her she said good-day to you. Even so, the boys never
could seem to get up the nerve to go over and talk with her, and most of the time she
simply looked through them, even when they tomcatted up and down the street trying
to get her eye. They wrestled, played Tarzan, did foolheaded bicycle tricks. It was a
sorry business. A great many girls in town strolled by the Sawyer house two and three   20

NOTES

line

2 **the way boys do**　do = smell all sour and sweet
3 **You're s'posed to**　s'posed = supposed. be supposed to ~「～することになっている、普通は～する」。
4 **folks** = people
4 **lilting**（形）「軽快な」
5 **drifting in the air delicate as the music**　drifting in the air は分詞構文で a night moth を修飾、「空気の中を漂って」。delicate as the music も同様に a night moth を修飾。
7 **doubled up** > double up「二つ折りになる」
8 **grubby boy-eyes**　grubby = dirty, grimy. boy を修飾。
8 **twitching** > twitch「びくっと動く」ここでは、ろうそくの様にきらきらと揺らめく。
9 **dickens**「いたずらっこ、小僧」ここでは小さな娘、ミス・ボビットのこと。
9 **gee, to hell with it**「ああ、ちくしょう」gee は「おや、まあ、ちぇっ」などの意。to hell は強調などで使われる。
13 **thanking her for the flowers**　a note を修飾。
14 **to beat the band**「群を抜いて」
15 **Webster's dictionary**「ウェブスター辞書」Noah Webster (1785–1843) はアメリカの辞書編集者・教育者。
17 **get up the nerve to**「～する勇気を出す」この nerve は「勇気、度胸」。
18 **tomcatted** > tomcat（動）「（男性が女性の後などを）追いかけまわす、気を引く」
18 **up and down the street**　up and down「上下に、あちこちへ、すみずみまで」
19 **played Tarzan** > play Tarzan「ターザンごっこをする」
19 **foolheaded bicycle tricks**「ばかげた自転車の技」
20 **sorry business**「あわれなこと、情けないありさま」
20 **strolled by** > stroll by「～のあたりをぶらつく」

times within an hour just on the chance of getting a look. Some of the girls who did this were: Cora McCall, Mary Murphy Jones, Janice Ackerman. Miss Bobbit did not show any interest in them either. Cora would not speak to Billy Bob any more. The same was true with Janice and Preacher. As a matter of fact, Janice wrote Preacher a letter in red ink on lace-trimmed paper in which she told him he was vile beyond all 25 human beings and words, that she considered their engagement broken, that he could have back the stuffed squirrel he'd given her. Preacher, saying he wanted to act nice, stopped her the next time she passed our house, and said, well, hell, she could keep that old squirrel if she wanted to. Afterwards, he couldn't understand why Janice ran away bawling the way she did. 30

Then one day the boys were being crazier than usual; Billy Bob was sagging around in his daddy's World War khakis, and Preacher, stripped to the waist, had a naked woman drawn on his chest with one of Aunt El's old lipsticks. They looked like perfect fools, but Miss Bobbit, reclining in a swing, merely yawned. It was noon, and there was no one passing in the street, except a colored girl, baby-fat and sugar-plum 35 shaped, who hummed along carrying a pail of blackberries. But the boys, teasing at her like gnats, joined hands and wouldn't let her go by, not until she paid a tariff. I ain't studyin' no tariff, she said, what kinda tariff you talkin' about, mister? A party in the barn, said Preacher, between clenched teeth, mighty nice party in the barn. And she, with a sulky shrug, said, huh, she intended studyin' no barn parties. Whereupon 40 Billy Bob capsized her berry pail, and when she, with despairing, piglike shrieks, bent down in futile gestures of rescue, Preacher, who can be mean as the devil, gave her behind a kick which sent her sprawling jellylike among the blackberries and the dust. Miss Bobbit came tearing across the road, her finger wagging like a metronome; like a schoolteacher she clapped her hands, stamped her foot, said: "It is a well- 45 known fact that gentlemen are put on the face of this earth for the protection of ladies. Do you suppose boys behave this way in towns like Memphis, New York, London, Hollywood or Paris?" The boys hung back, and shoved their hands in their pockets. Miss Bobbit helped the colored girl to her feet; she dusted her off, dried her eyes, held out a handkerchief and told her to blow. "A pretty pass," she said, "a fine situation 50 when a lady can't walk safely in the public daylight."

23 **would not speak**「絶対に話そうとしなかった」この would は過去における強い意志・主張。

25 **lace-trimmed paper**「レースの縁取りをした便せん」

25 **beyond all human beings and words**「どんな人間より、どんな言葉でも言えないくらい」

26 **considered their engagement broken**　consider A B「A を B だとみなす、判断する」

27 **stuffed squirrel**「リスのはく製」stuffed = stuff（動）「詰め物をする、はく製にする」の過去分詞。squirrel [skw'ɚːrəl]。

27 **act nice**「まっとうに振る舞う、きちんと対応する」

28 **stopped her** > stop her「彼女を呼び止める」

28 **well, hell,**「なあ、あのさ」

30 **bawling** > bawl [bɔːl]　= cry loud.（動）「大声で泣く」。

31 **sagging around** > sag around「（服のすそなどを）だらしなく垂れさせる、ぶかぶかに着込む」

32 **World War khakis**「大戦中の軍服」

32 **stripped to the waist**「腰まで服をはだけて」

32 **had a naked woman drawn**「裸の女性の絵を描いて」have A B「A を B（の状態）にして」。have の使役用法。drawn は draw（動）「描く」の過去分詞。

34 **swing**（名）「ぶらんこ」

34 **yawned** > yawn [jɔːn]「あくびをする」

35 **a colored girl**「黒人の娘」colored は「有色人種の、黒人の」という意味で、しばしば差別的な意味で使用されていた。今日では使ってはいけない。

35 **baby-fat**「赤ん坊みたいにぽっちゃりして」

35 **sugar-plum shaped**「シュガープラムみたいに丸い」sugar-plum は球形の砂糖菓子、キャンディー。

36 **hummed** > hum [hʌm]（動）「鼻歌を歌う、ハミングする」

36 **a pail of blackberries**「ひと山の、バケツ一杯のブラックベリー」

37 **gnat** [næt]「ぶよ（吸血性の昆虫）」

37 **tariff**「通行税」

38 **ain't studyin'**「〜なんてどうでもいい」ain't = am not の短縮形、会話で使われる。studyin' などはこの土地特有の発音を表すために短縮形で記述されている。

38 **kinda** = kind of

38 **mister**　20 世紀半ばの南部では、黒人と白人の間の segregation（社会的分離）が存在した。子ども同士であっても、黒人から白人へは敬称が使われた。

39 **barn**「納屋」

39 **clenched**（形）「くいしばった、噛みしめた」

39 **mighty**（形）「格別の、ものすごい」

40 **whereupon**（非制限用法）「そこで、それから」

41 **capsized** > capsize [kæp'saɪz]（動）「ひっくり返す」

41 **berry pail**「ベリーを入れたバケツ」

41 **with despairing, piglike shrieks**　挿入句で、she を修飾。「絶望的な、豚みたいな叫び声をあげて」。

42 **futile** [fjuːtaɪl, fjuːtl]（形）「効果のない、無駄な」

43 **sprawling jellylike among**「〜のなかにゼリーみたいにはいつくばって」

44 **come tearing**「ものすごい勢いでやってくる」tearing は会話表現の形容詞「猛烈な、すさまじい」。

44 **wagging** > wag（動）「（人が指を）振る」

46 **gentlemen are put on the face of this earth for the protection of ladies**「紳士というのは淑女を守るためにこの地球上にあるのです」アメリカ南部では騎士道精神に基づいた女性を守り敬う伝統があった。ただし、同時に男性と女性の行動範囲や自由に大きな差があった。

48 **shoved** > shove「押す、（ぞんざいに）ねじこむ」

49 **helped the colored girl to her feet**「その黒人の娘を立たせてあげた」

49 **dusted her off** > dust her off「彼女についたほこりを払う」

50 **"A pretty pass," she said, "a fine situation when a lady can't walk safely in the public daylight."**
直訳すると、「『素敵な道ですこと』と彼女は言った。『昼日中にレディが安全に歩くこともできないなんてすばらしいことですね』」。だが、ここでは皮肉で言っていて、反対のことを意味している。

EXERCISES

Q1. Choose the most suitable word to each blank in the following summary from the word list blow.

The narrator tells us that his cousin Billy Bob comes to his room. Billy Bob is very worried about Miss Bobbit and doesn't seem at all sorry that he cut all of his mother's roses. He claims that it is (1) to send flowers to sick people. The narrator and Billy Bob hear music from the victrola across the street but cannot see if Miss Bobbit is (2). Billy Bob seems to be lovesick. Preacher is also in love with Miss Bobbit. Miss Bobbit sits on the front porch for all to see, but she ignores the boys. They continue to perform in front of the boarding house but are afraid to visit her. Cora stops (3) to Billy Bob and Preacher and Janice break off their engagement. One morning, Billy Bob and Preacher are performing crazy tricks in front of the boarding house when a black girl carrying a pail of berries passes by. The two boys (4) her. Billy Bob tips over her pail of berries, and Preacher (5) her. She falls into the dust. Miss Bobbit rushes into the street and scolds the boys for their rude behavior. The boys are ashamed.

[speaking, dancing, bully, kicks, proper]

Q2. Mark the following sentences true (T) or false (F) according to the story. If it's false, correct it.

1. Billy Bob thinks it was okay to steal his mother's roses because Miss Bobbit is sick, and you are supposed to give roses to sick people.   [   ]

2. Billy Bob regrets picking all of his mother's roses.   [   ]

3. Miss Bobbit divides her attention equally between Billy Bob and Preacher.

[   ]

4. Miss Bobbit thanks Aunt El for the roses in a note.   [   ]

5. Janice breaks off her engagement to Preacher because he is only interested in Miss Bobbit.   [   ]

6. Preacher uses Aunt El's lipstick to draw on Billy Bob.   [   ]

7. Billy Bob and Preacher steal berries from a girl passing on the street. [   ]

8. Miss Bobbit scolds the boys by contrasting their rude behavior with boys in cities
   such as New York and Paris.   [   ]

Q3. Match definition 1–8 with the appropriate word or phrase below.

1. open your mouth wide and breathe in deeply through it, usually because you are
   tired or bored.   (   )

2. to cry loudly, especially in an unpleasant and annoying way.   (   )

3. people in general.   (   )

4. to walk somewhere in a slow, relaxed way.   (   )

5. to push in a rough way.   (   )

6. to the greatest possible degree, the best.   (   )

7. in a way that you think is morally acceptable or fair.   (   )

8. having no purpose because there is no chance of success.   (   )

[bawl, folk, futile, shove, stroll, to beat the band, righteously, yawn]

Q4. Choose the most suitable word or phrase from the list above to fill in the blanks. If necessary, correct the word form.

1. They believed they were fighting (   ) in defense of their country.

2. It's raining (   ). We'd better stay home today.

3. Like most (   ), I enjoy a good meal.

4. Their efforts to revive him were (   ).

5. The crowd was pushing and (   ) to get a better view.

6. A child is (   ) for more food.

7. People were (   ) along the beach.

8. We couldn't help (   ) during the speech.

UNIT **6**

the 11th and 12th paragraphs

Warm Up

Recite the following sentences out loud.

> 1. My cousin and I were never far apart those days.
> 2. You have our support whatever you decide.
> 3. He was so confident that there was nothing to do but agree with his plan.
> 4. People gave the old man bows to show their respect.
> 5. Don't try to give any advice to the child. That is not your business.

Then the two of them went back and sat on Mrs. Sawyer's porch; and for the next year they were never far apart, Miss Bobbit and this baby elephant, whose name was Rosalba Cat. At first, Mrs. Sawyer raised a fuss about Rosalba being so much at her house. She told Aunt El that it went against the grain to have a nigger lolling smack there in plain sight on her front porch. But Miss Bobbit had a certain magic, 5 whatever she did she did it with completeness, and so directly, so solemnly, that there was nothing to do but accept it. For instance, the tradespeople in town used to snicker when they called her *Miss Bobbit*; but by and by she was Miss Bobbit, and they gave her stiff little bows as she whirled by spinning her parasol. Miss Bobbit told everyone that Rosalba was her sister, which caused a good many jokes; but 10 like most of her ideas, it gradually seemed natural, and when we would overhear them calling each other Sister Rosalba and Sister Bobbit none of us cracked a smile. But Sister Rosalba and Sister Bobbit did some queer things. There was the business about the dogs. Now there are a great many dogs in this town, rat terriers, bird dogs, bloodhounds; they trail along the forlorn noon-hot streets in sleepy herds of six to a 15 dozen, all waiting only for dark and the moon, when straight through the lonesome hours you can hear them howling: someone is dying, someone is dead. Miss Bobbit complained to the Sheriff; she said that certain of the dogs always planted themselves under her window, and that she was a light sleeper to begin with; what is more, and as

NOTES

line

1 **the two of them** =Miss Bobbit and Rosalba.

2 **this baby elephant** Rosalba の様子を指している。

3 **raised a fuss** > raise a fuss「大騒ぎをする」fuss（名）「興奮、騒ぎ」。

4 **against the grain**「（気質、性分）に反している」

4 **nigger** 黒人に対する蔑称として使われていた語。今日では特定の状況を除いて差別語としてみなされており、決して使ってはいけない。コラム参照。

4 **lolling smack** = relaxing right in front of ~. loll「だらりとくつろぐ」smack「～の前で（強調）」。

6 **whatever she did she did it with ~** whatever she did のあとにカンマ (,) を補って考えるとよい。

6 **and so directly, so solemnly, that ~** so that 構文。

7 **there was nothing to do but accept it** there is nothing but ~「～するしかない、かならず～することになる」

7 **tradespeople**「商人」

8 **snicker**「くすくす笑う、忍び笑いする」

8 **by and by**「やがて、まもなく」

8 **she was Miss Bobbit** ここではイタリックでなくなっていることに注目。皆が笑いもせず、ごく自然に Miss Bobbit と呼ぶようになったことを表す。

9 **whirled by** > whirl by「足早に通りすぎる」

10 **…, which caused ~**「…した。そのことは～を引き起こした」関係代名詞 which の非制限用法。

12 **cracked a smile** > crack a smile「笑みをもらす」

13 **queer** [kwɪə(r)]「奇妙な、おかしな」

13 **the business**「（ある）こと、出来事」

14 **rat terriers, bird dogs, bloodhounds**「ラットテリア（ネズミ捕りの犬）、バードドッグ（鳥猟犬）、ブラッドハウンド（嗅覚の鋭い中・大型犬）」

15 **forlorn**「わびしい、人気のない」

15 **herds** > herd [hɜːd]「（動物などの）群れ」

15 **six to a dozen**「6 匹から 12 匹（1 ダース）ほど」

16 **lonesome**「一人ぼっちの、わびしい」

17 **howling** > howl [haʊl]「吠える」

17 **someone is dying, someone is dead.** 犬が鳴くのは誰かが死んでいることを示すという迷信がある。

18 **planted** > plant（動）「植えつける、居すわる」

Sister Rosalba said, she did not believe they were dogs at all, but some kind of devil. 20
Naturally the Sheriff did nothing; and so she took the matter into her own hands. One
morning, after an especially loud night, she was seen stalking through the town with
Rosalba at her side, Rosalba carrying a flower basket filled with rocks; whenever they
saw a dog they paused while Miss Bobbit scrutinized him. Sometimes she would
shake her head, but more often she said, "Yes, that's one of them, Sister Rosalba," 25
and Sister Rosalba, with ferocious aim, would take a rock from her basket and crack
the dog between the eyes.

18 Another thing that happened concerns Mr. Henderson. Mr. Henderson has a back
room in the Sawyer house; a tough runt of a man who formerly was a wildcat oil
prospector in Oklahoma, he is about seventy years old and, like a lot of old men, 30
obsessed by functions of the body. Also, he is a terrible drunk. One time he had been
drunk for two weeks; whenever he heard Miss Bobbit and Sister Rosalba moving
around the house, he would charge to the top of the stairs and bellow down to Mrs.
Sawyer that there were midgets in the walls trying to get at his supply of toilet paper.
They've already stolen fifteen cents' worth, he said. One evening, when the two girls 35
were sitting under a tree in the yard, Mr. Henderson, sporting nothing more than a
nightshirt, stamped out after them. Steal all my toilet paper; will you? he hollered, I'll
show you midgets .... Somebody come help me, else these midget bitches are liable
to make off with every sheet in town. It was Billy Bob and Preacher who caught Mr.
Henderson and held him until some grown men arrived and began to tie him up. Miss 40
Bobbit, who had behaved with admirable calm, told the men they did not know how
to tie a proper knot, and undertook to do so herself. She did such a good job that all
the circulation stopped in Mr. Henderson's hands and feet and it was a month before
he could walk again.

人種に関する差別的な言葉について

1940 年代のアメリカ南部を舞台としたこの "Children on Their Birthdays" では、現在で
は差別的とみなされる行動や言葉がみられます。たとえば、Mrs. Sawyer は黒人の Rosalba
Cat が彼女の家の敷地に出入りしていることに憤慨し、"it went against the grain to have
a nigger lolling smack there in plain sight on her front porch" と言っています。ここで使
われている、n で始まる差別語、いわゆる N-word は、今日ではきわめて軽蔑的な言葉

21 **naturally**「自然に、当然、もちろん」

21 **took the matter into her own hands**「彼女自身でなんとかすることにした」matter（名）「こと、問題」。

22 **stalking** > stalk [stɔːk]「こっそり追跡する、ストーキングする」

23 **Rosalba carrying**　分詞構文、先行部と主語が異なる。「ロザルバが〜して」。

24 **scrutinized** > scrutinize [skruːtənaɪz]「精査する、じろじろ見る」

25 **one of them** = one of the devils

26 **ferocious** [fəˈrəʊʃəs]「おそろしい、狂暴な」

26 **crack**「激しくぶつける、砕く」

28 **concerns** > concern（動）「〜に関係する、〜に関する」

28 **back room**「屋敷の裏手の部屋」

29 **runt**「発育不良の動物、または人」

29 **wildcat oil prospector**「一匹狼の石油の試掘者」wildcat は「無謀な、危険な」、また「石油が出るかどうか不明な地域で試掘をする個人探鉱者」の意味がある。

30 **Oklahoma**「オクラホマ」アメリカ中南部。20 世紀に油田が発見された。

31 **obsessed by**「〜に取りつかれた、〜のことばかり気にする」

31 **functions of the body**「体の諸機能（おもに健康について）」

31 **drunk**（名）「酔っぱらい」

33 **bellow**「わめく、どなる」

34 **midgets** > midget「ちび、小人」蔑称として使われるので注意。

34 **supply**（名）「在庫、蓄え」

35 **fifteen cents' worth**「15 セント分」

36 **sporting** > sport（動）「（衣装などを）身につける、着る」

37 **stamped out** > stamp out「足を踏みつける、荒々しい足取りで進む」

37 **hollered** > holler「大声を上げる、わめく」

38 **else**（副）「さもないと」

38 **these midget bitches**「この小娘ども」bitch は女性に対する蔑称。

38 **are liable to** > be liable to（アメリカ方言）「〜しがちな、たぶん〜する」

39 **make off with**「〜を持ち去る、盗む」

39 **It was Billy Bob and Preacher who ~**「〜したのはビリー・ボブとプリーチャーだった」強調構文。

41 **they did not know how to tie a proper knot**「あなたたちはちゃんとした縄の結び方も知らない」they = some grown men.

42 **undertook** > undertake「引き受ける、請け負う」

42 **She did such a good job that ~**　such … that ~「とても…なので〜」

43 **circulation** [sɜːkjəˈleɪʃn]「（血などの）循環」

43 **it was a month before ~**「〜するまでに 1 カ月かかった」

であり、決して使ってはいけない言葉となっています。ただし、黒人文化の中では、むしろ仲間の間での親愛の情や自分たちの連帯を表すために使われたりもしています。Hip-Hop やラップなどの歌詞でこうした言葉が使われるのを耳にしたことがある人もいるかもしれませんね。ですが、こうした文化やコミュニティの外にいる人間が使う時は、決して同じ意味を持つことにはなりません。言葉は時代や環境、文化の中で生まれ、変化し、特定の意味を持って使われます。言葉のうしろにあるそうした背景を知り、理解することも、外国語を学び、コミュニケーションをとっていく上でとても重要なことです。

Q1. Choose the most suitable word to each blank in the following summary from the word list blow.

Miss Bobbit takes Rosalba Cat to the front porch of the boarding house and they (1) close friends. Miss Bobbit claims Rosalba is her sister and they begin calling each other Sister Rosalba and Sister Bobbit. Stray dogs disturb Miss Bobbit's sleep by (2) under her window. Together, Miss Bobbit and Rosalba hunt down and (3) the stray dogs. Mr. Henderson, an alcoholic living in the boarding house, (4) Miss Bobbit and Rosalba. He accuses them of stealing his toilet paper. Several boys defend the girls and then some grown men try to tie up Mr. Henderson. Miss Bobbit complains that the men don't know how to tie knots. She takes over and ties up Mr. Henderson. She (5) him up so tightly that he cannot walk for a month.

[howling, kill, attacks, ties, become]

Q2. Mark the following sentences true (T) or false (F) according to the story. If it's false, correct it.

1. The narrator compares Rosalba to a baby elephant because she is fat.   [   ]

2. Mrs. Sawyer doesn't want Rosalba in her house because she eats too much.

     [   ]

3. Miss Bobbit defends Rosalba by claiming she is her sister.   [   ]

4. Miss Bobbit and Rosalba collect stray dogs and take them to the Sheriff. [   ]

5. Mr. Henderson rents a room in the same house as Miss Bobbit and her mother.

     [   ]

6. Mr. Henderson used to work in Texas.   [   ]

7. Mr. Henderson plays a joke on Miss Bobbit and Rosalba.   [   ]

8. Miss Bobbit ties up Mr. Henderson so tightly that he cannot walk for a month.

     [   ]

Q3. Match definition 1–8 with the appropriate word or phrase below.

1. to look at or examine somebody or something carefully. (   )

2. to constantly think about something until it is overwhelming. (   )

3. the movement of blood around the body. (   )

4. not cared for and with no people. (   )

5. before long; soon. (   )

6. having qualities that you praise and respect. (   )

7. to involve somebody or something. (   )

8. to laugh in a quiet unpleasant way, especially at somebody's mistakes.

(   )

[admirable, by and by, circulation, concern,
forlorn, scrutinize, snicker, obsess]

Q4. Choose the most suitable word or phrase from the list above to fill in the blanks. If necessary, correct the word form.

1. The letter is for both of us, but it mainly (   ) you.

2. Regular exercise will improve blood (   ).

3. (   ) she met the old man she had been looking for.

4. He made his points with (   ) clarity.

5. The cottage stood (   ) and empty.

6. Although his friends (   ), they did not correct him.

7. The statement was carefully (   ) before publication.

8. He's (   ) by video games.

UNIT **7**

●●

the 13th and 14th paragraphs

19

Warm Up

Recite the following sentences out loud.

> 1. It was shortly afterwards that I noticed that I left my wallet.
> 2. The smell was so offensive that I couldn't eat.
> 3. He has enough experience in scuba diving to teach a class on it.
> 4. As a matter of fact, I really liked the new office.
> 5. The trouble with her was that she was too generous.

20

It was shortly afterwards that Miss Bobbit paid us a call. She came on Sunday and I was there alone, the family having gone to church. "The odors of a church are so offensive," she said, leaning forward and with her hands folded primly before her. "I don't want you to think I'm a heathen, Mr. C. I've had enough experience to know that there is a God and that there is a Devil. But the way to tame the Devil is 5 not to go down there to church and listen to what a sinful mean fool he is. No, love the Devil like you love Jesus: because he is a powerful man, and will do you a good turn if he knows you trust him. He has frequently done me good turns, like at dancing school in Memphis . . . . I always called in the Devil to help me get the biggest part in our annual show. That is common sense; you see, I knew Jesus wouldn't have any 10 truck with dancing. Now, as a matter of fact, I have called in the Devil just recently. He is the only one who can help me get out of this town. Not that I live here, not exactly. I think always about somewhere else, somewhere else where everything is dancing, like people dancing in the streets, and everything is pretty, like children on their birthdays. My precious papa said I live in the sky, but if he'd lived more in the 15 sky he'd be rich like he wanted to be. The trouble with my papa was he did not love the Devil, he let the Devil love him. But I am very smart in that respect; I know the next best thing is very often the best. It was the next best thing for us to move to this town; and since I can't pursue my career here, the next best thing for me is to start a little business on the side. Which is what I have done. I am sole subscription agent in 20

NOTES

line

1 **It was shortly afterwards that ~**「～したのはそのすぐ後だった」It … that~ 構文。

1 **paid us a call** > pay a call「訪問する」

2 **the family having gone to church**　分詞構文。先行詞が前半の文章と異なる。また、この時代の南部で、日曜に教会に行かないというのはかなり異常だった。特に子どもの場合。

2 **odor** [əʊdər]「におい」

3 **primly** (副)「堅苦しく、取り澄まして」

4 **heathen** [hiːðn]「(キリスト教から見て) 異教徒、不信心者」

5 **Mr. C**　=語り手。作者のCapoteと同じイニシャルであることに注意。

5 **tame** [teɪm] (動)「飼いならす、手なずける」

6 **a sinful mean fool**「罪深いいやしいおろか者」mean (形)「いやしい、下品な」。

7 **Jesus**「ジーザス」=イエス・キリスト。

7 **a good turn**「幸運」turn (名)「機会、好機」。

9 **called in** > call in「呼ぶ、援助を求める」

10 **annual** [ænjuəl]「年一度の、例年の」

10 **common sense**「常識」

10 **have any truck with** > have a truck with「～と取引する、～と関係がある」truck「(通例否定文で) 交渉、関係」。

12 **Not that I live here**「私はここに住んでいるわけではない」not that ~「～ということではない」。

14 **children on their birthdays**　この短編のタイトル、またミス・ボビットの理想を表している。

15 **I live in the sky**　sky = 天国、または夢の世界。

17 **let the Devil love him**　let A do「A に～させる」。

17 **the next best thing**「二番目に最善のこと、次善の策」

20 **on the side**「副業として、それとは別に」

20 **Which** = 前の文の to start a little business を受けている。

20 **subscription agent**「定期購読の取扱業者」

this county for an impressive list of magazines, including *Reader's Digest*, *Popular Mechanics*, *Dime Detective* and *Child's Life*. To be sure, Mr. C., I'm not here to sell you anything. But I have a thought in mind. I was thinking those two boys that are always hanging around here, it occurred to me that they are men, after all. Do you suppose they would make a pair of likely assistants?" 25

Billy Bob and Preacher worked hard for Miss Bobbit, and for Sister Rosalba, too. Sister Rosalba carried a line of cosmetics called Dewdrop, and it was part of the boys' job to deliver purchases to her customers. Billy Bob used to be so tired in the evening he could hardly chew his supper. Aunt El said it was a shame and a pity, and finally one day when Billy Bob came down with a touch of sunstroke she said, all right, that 30 settled it, Billy Bob would just have to quit Miss Bobbit. But Billy Bob cussed her out until his daddy had to lock him in his room; whereupon he said he was going to kill himself. Some cook we'd had told him once that if you ate a mess of collards all slopped over with molasses it would kill you sure as shooting; and so that is what he did. I'm dying, he said, rolling back and forth on his bed, I'm dying and nobody 35 cares.

21 ***Reader's Digest, Popular Mechanics, Dime Detective* and *Child's Life*** 当時人気だった雑誌。*Reader's Digest* は大衆雑誌の記事の要約を中心とした雑誌、*Popular Mechanics* は通俗科学技術雑誌、*Dime Detective* は大衆向けミステリー小説、*Child's Life* は子ども向け雑誌。

22 **I'm not here to ~**「〜をしにきているわけではない」

24 **hanging around** > hang around「つきまとう、うろつく」

25 **likely assistants**「アシスタント候補」likely (副)「〜に適当な、〜できる」。

27 **Dewdrop**「デュウドロップ」化粧品ブランドの名前。

28 **purchases** > purchase (名)「購入品」

28 **so tired in the evening** このあとの that が省略されている。

29 **chew** [tʃuː]「(食べ物などを)かむ」

29 **a shame and a pity**「情けないしあわれなこと」

30 **a touch of sunstroke**「すこし日射病気味になって」a touch of ~「〜気味になる」。

30 **that settled it**「これで決まりだね」settle (動)「決定する」

31 **quit Miss Bobitt**「ミス・ボビットの仕事をするのをやめる」quit「やめる、離れる」。

31 **cussed** > cuss「ののしる、毒づく」

33 **Some cook we'd had**「僕たちがむかし雇っていたある料理人」cook (名)「料理人」。そのあとの that が省略されている。we'd had = we had had.

33 **a mess of collards all slopped over with molasses**「糖蜜をたっぷりかけたコラードを一皿」collard「コラード(ケールの一種)」、slop (動)「(液体を)こぼす、かける」、molasses「糖蜜」。

34 **sure as shooting**「銃で撃つのと同じくらい確実に」

"a shame" (p. 38, l. 29)

本文での shame はその後 and a pity と続くように、"used to say that something is a cause for feeling sad or disappointed" の意味で、pity と synonym です。What a shame! が「全く気の毒だ(残念だ)」の意味で What a pity!「(実に)かわいそうだ；それは残念だ」と似ています。

　しかし、shame「面目を失ったことに対する屈辱感」や「他人に見下されて感じる恥辱」の意味でも使われ、disgrace や dishonor と同義語で、基本的に「(罪意識・不品行などによって生ずる)恥ずかしさ」や「(倫理・道徳上)不名誉なこと」に言及するものです。

　一方で、pity「自分より下か弱い者の苦痛や不幸を見て感じる悲しみ」で compassion や sympathy と同義語になります。

　shame を「恥」としたことから生じた誤解も多くあり、例えば、人に褒められたとき、日本語では「恥ずかしい」と言うことがありますが、英語では謝辞を述べる方が普通です。子供などが人前で「恥ずかしがる」のは、shame や ashamed ではなく、be shy または be bashful などとなります。

　一方、「質問に答えられなくて恥をかいた」と言う日本語表現の場合、宗教的・倫理的に違反行為をしたわけではないので、質問をされて答えにくいなどのこうした場合は be embarrassed/bewildered などを用います。

EXERCISES

Q1. Choose the most suitable word to each blank in the following summary from the word list blow.

Miss Bobbit visits the narrator and explains her philosophy about God and the Devil. She (1) in being friendly with the Devil so he will do her favors. Miss Bobbit claims she often (2) herself in a place where everything is pretty, like children on their birthdays. She has a magazine subscription business and wants to (3) Billy Bob and Preacher to work for her. Billy Bob and Preacher become Miss Bobbit's assistants. In addition to the magazines, they also deliver cosmetics for Sister Rosalba. Billy Bob works so hard that he (4) from sunstroke. Billy Bob fights with his mother, who tells him he has to (5) his job because he is working too hard. Billy Bob locks himself in his room and complains that he is dying.

[quit, imagines, suffers, believes, hire]

Q2. Mark the following sentences true (T) or false (F) according to the story. If it's false, correct it.

1. Mr. C is the narrator. [　]

2. Miss Bobbit does not believe in God. [　]

3. Miss Bobbit asks the Devil for help when she wants something. [　]

4. Miss Bobbit uses the phrase, "like children on their birthdays" to describe a place where everything is pretty. [　]

5. Billy Bob and Preacher refused to work for Rosalba. [　]

6. Billy Bob was almost too tired to eat in the evenings from working so hard.
[　]

7. Billy Bob was happy to quit his job because it was too much work for a young boy.
[　]

8. Billy Bob tries to commit suicide by eating collards and molasses. [　]

Q3. Match definition 1–8 with the appropriate word or phrase below.

1. an amount of money that you pay to receive regular copies of a newspaper or magazine. ( )

2. happening or done once every year. ( )

3. something obtained especially for a price. ( )

4. a small amount of. ( )

5. to train an animal or person into being cooperative. ( )

6. promising, capable. ( )

7. a smell, especially one that is unpleasant. ( )

8. in this era, an offensive word for non-Christians. ( )

[annual, a touch of, heathen, likely, odor, purchase, subscription, tame]

Q4. Choose the most suitable word or phrase from the list above to fill in the blanks. If necessary, correct the word form.

1. He was able to ( ) his dog so it wouldn't bite strangers.

2. The 12th ( ) Music Festival starts on Friday the 25th.

3. He noticed the stale ( ) of cigarette smoke.

4. Don't forget to renew the ( ) of our magazine.

5. The church set out to convert the ( ).

6. Everyone thought he was a ( ) boy who would succeed at his job.

7. Her latest ( ) was a long black coat.

8. She noticed ( ) garlic in the sauce.

UNIT **8**

....

the 15th, 16th and 17th paragraphs

22
Warm Up

Recite the following sentences out loud.

> 1. There's nothing wrong with you, so don't worry.
> 2. He did something that surprised all his colleagues.
> 3. She didn't know whether she should go or stay.
> 4. She decided to leave the children alone and let them do anything they wanted.
> 5. He was very honest about his capacity to work.

23
  Miss Bobbit came over and told him to hush up. "There's nothing wrong with you, boy," she said. "All you've got is a stomach ache." Then she did something that shocked Aunt El very much: she stripped the covers off Billy Bob and rubbed him down with alcohol from head to toe. When Aunt El told her she did not think that was a nice thing for a little girl to do, Miss Bobbit replied: "I don't know whether it's 5 nice or not, but it's certainly very refreshing." After which Aunt El did all she could to keep Billy Bob from going back to work for her, but his daddy said to leave him alone, they would have to let the boy lead his own life.

24
  Miss Bobbit was very honest about money. She paid Billy Bob and Preacher their exact commission, and she would never let them treat her, as they often tried to do, at 10 the drugstore or to the picture show. "You'd better save your money," she told them. "That is, if you want to go to college. Because neither one of you has got the brains to win a scholarship, not even a football scholarship." But it was over money that Billy Bob and Preacher had a big falling out; that was not the real reason, of course: the real reason was that they had grown cross-eyed jealous over Miss Bobbit. So one day, and 15 he had the gall to do this right in front of Billy Bob, Preacher said to Miss Bobbit that she'd better check her accounts carefully because he had more than a suspicion that Billy Bob wasn't turning over to her *all* the money he collected. That's a damned lie, said Billy Bob, and with a clean left hook he knocked Preacher off the Sawyer porch

NOTES

1 **hush up**「静かにする、だまる」

1 **There's nothing wrong with you**「あなたにはなにも問題はない、あなたどこも悪くはない」

3 **rubbed him down** > rub ~ down「(体を) 上から下までこする、マッサージする」

6 **After which** which はそれより前に起きた出来事全体を指す。

7 **leave him alone** > leave ~ alone「〜の好きにさせておく」

8 **lead his own life** > lead one's own life「自分の人生を自分で選ぶ」

10 **commission**「手数料、歩合」

10 **treat**「〜 (人) をもてなす、〜におごる」

11 **drugstore**「ドラッグストア」アメリカのドラッグストアは薬以外の商品も扱い、軽食を取ることもできる。

11 **picture show** = movie or cinema.「映画館」。

11 **You'd better** had better は強い勧告。「〜しないとだめよ」。

12 **That is**「つまり」= that is to say

13 **scholarship**「奨学金」

13 **football** (米)「アメリカンフットボール」

13 **it was over money that** it ~that ... 構文。「...したのはお金をめぐってだった」。

14 **falling out**「(親しかった人たちの間の) 仲たがい」

15 **cross-eyed** (話)「(考え方などが) 異常な」形容詞的用法。

16 **he had the gall to** = he had the nerve to (話)「彼は厚かましくも〜した」

17 **accounts** > account「勘定、収支計算書」

18 **turning over** > turn over「引き渡す」

18 **all the money** all がイタリックで強調されていることに注意。「お金のすべては (渡していない)」= 一部を自分のものにしている、という意味。

18 **collected** > collect (動)「集める、集金する」

18 **damned** (形) (話)「ひどい、まったくの」

19 **a clean left hook**「きれいにきまった左フック」パンチ。

19 **knocked Preacher off the Sawyer porch**「プリーチャーをソーヤー家のポーチから突き落とした」

and jumped after him into a bed of nasturtiums. But once Preacher got a hold on him, 20
Billy Bob didn't stand a chance. Preacher even rubbed dirt in his eyes. During all
this, Mrs. Sawyer, leaning out an upper-story window, screamed like an eagle, and
Sister Rosalba; fatly cheerful, ambiguously shouted, Kill him! Kill him! Kill him!
Only Miss Bobbit seemed to know what she was doing. She plugged in the lawn
hose, and gave the boys a closeup, blinding bath. Gasping, Preacher staggered to his 25
feet. Oh, honey, he said, shaking himself like a wet dog, honey, you've got to decide.
"Decide *what?*" said Miss Bobbit, right away in a huff. Oh, honey, wheezed Preacher,
you don't want us boys killing each other. You got to decide who is your real true
sweetheart. "Sweetheart, my eye," said Miss Bobbit. "I should've known better than
to get myself involved with a lot of country children. What sort of businessman are 30
you going to make? Now, you listen here, Preacher Star: I don't want a sweetheart,
and if I did, it wouldn't be you. As a matter of fact, you don't even get up when a lady
enters the room."

Preacher spit on the ground and swaggered over to Billy Bob. Come on, he said,
just as though nothing had happened, she's a hard one, she is, she don't want nothing 35
but to make trouble between two good friends. For a moment it looked as if Billy Bob
was going to join him in a peaceful togetherness; but suddenly, coming to his senses,
he drew back and made a gesture. The boys regarded each other a full minute, all the
closeness between them turning an ugly color: you can't hate so much unless you
love, too. And Preacher's face showed all of this. But there was nothing for him to do 40
except go away. Oh, yes, Preacher, you looked so lost that day that for the first time I
really liked you, so skinny and mean and lost going down the road all by yourself.

20　**a bed of nasturtiums**「キンレンカの花壇」キンレンカはあざやかなオレンジの花。bed「花壇」。

21　**stand a chance**「勝ち目がある」chance「見込み、勝算」。

21　**dirt** [dɜ:t]「泥、よごれ」

22　**leaning out** > lean out「身を乗り出す」

22　**upper-story**「上の階」story（名）「階層、階」。

23　**ambiguously** [æmˈbɪɡjuəsli]（副）「どうにも解釈できる、不明瞭に」二人のうちどちらに対して言っているのかはっきりしないが、という意味。

24　**lawn hose**「芝生用のホース」

25　**a closeup, blinding bath**「至近距離から目が見えなくなるほどの放水」

25　**Gasping,**　分詞構文。「息を詰まらせながら、〜」。

25　**staggered** > stagger「（よろめきながら）立つ」

26　**you've got to**「〜しないといけない」

27　**in a huff**「むっとして、腹を立てて」

27　**wheezed** > wheeze「ぜいぜいと息をする、息を切りながら言う」

28　**you don't want us boys killing ~**「ぼくらに殺し合いをしてほしくないだろう」want A ~ing「A に〜してほしい」。us boys は同格。

29　**sweetheart**「恋人、愛しい人」

29　**my eye**（話）「おやまあ、まったく」

29　**I should've known better than ~**「〜なんてするんじゃなかった」should have + 過去分詞「〜するべきだった」、仮定法過去完了の表現。know better than ~「〜する分別がある、〜するほどばかでない」。

30　**are you going to make**「（将来）〜になる」make「（人が）〜である、〜になる」。

32　**get up when a lady enters the room**「レディが部屋に入ってきた時に立ち上がる」南部の文化では、女性に対してこのように敬意を見せるのがよいとされた。

34　**spit**「つばを吐く」

34　**swaggered** > swagger「ふんぞりかえる、いばって見せる」

35　**as though** = as if「まるで〜かのように」

35　**a hard one**「ひどいやつ、冷たいやつ」

35　**she don't**　ただしくは she doesn't.

37　**coming to his senses** > come to one's senses「正気に戻る、われにかえる」

38　**made a gesture** > make a gesture「態度で示す」gesture「（自分の考えや感情をあらわす）身ぶり、しぐさ」。

38　**regarded each other a full minute**「たっぷり一分間お互いにらみあった」regard「（動）じっと見る」。

39　**turning ~**「〜になる」前半と主語が異なる分詞構文。

39　**you can't ~**　この you は「（一般的に）人は〜」。

40　**this** = その前の文全体を指す。

41　**except ~**「〜をのぞいて、〜する以外」

41　**so lost that day that ~**「あの日とても途方に暮れていた、だから〜」so that 構文。lost（形）「困り果てた、どうしたらいいかわからない」。

Q1. Choose the most suitable word to each blank in the following summary from the word list blow.

Miss Bobbit visits Billy Bob and (1) him a refreshing massage. Aunt El insists that Billy Bob should not return to work, but Billy Bob's father tells her to let Billy Bob make his own decisions. Billy Bob and Preacher have a fight. Preacher (2) Billy Bob of cheating Miss Bobbit, but they are actually jealous over Miss Bobbit's attention. Miss Bobbit (3) the boys with a garden hose to end the fight. Preacher insists that she should choose one of the boys as her sweetheart. Miss Bobbit says she has no (4) in either of them. Preacher tries to make up with Billy Bob and get him to leave Miss Bobbit. Billy Bob stays with Miss Bobbit, and Preacher (5), looking sad and lonely.

[sprays, leaves, interest, gives, accuses]

Q2. Mark the following sentences true (T) or false (F) according to the story. If it's false, correct it.

1. Miss Bobbit laughed at Billy Bob for trying to kill himself.   [   ]
2. Billy Bob's mother and father agree that he should not return to work.   [   ]
3. Billy Bob and Preacher treat Miss Bobbit at the drug store and cinema.   [   ]
4. Billy Bob and Preacher fight because they both want to be Miss Bobbit's sweetheart.
                                                                                    [   ]
5. Miss Bobbit doesn't want either boy for a sweetheart because they are country children with no manners.   [   ]
6. Preacher attempts to resolve his conflict with Billy Bob by blaming Miss Bobbit for their fight.   [   ]
7. Billy Bob accepts Preacher's apology after the fight.   [   ]
8. The narrator sympathizes with Preacher when he sees him all alone, without his friend, after the fight.   [   ]

Q3. Match definition 1–8 with the appropriate word or phrase below.

1. to walk in an extremely proud and confident way.   (   )

2. bring together from several places or from several people.   (   )

3. unclear, more than one possible interpretation.   (   )

4. to have the possibility of success.   (   )

5. money given by an organization to help pay for education. (   )

6. to be quiet; to stop talking or crying.   (   )

7. in other words.   (   )

8. a payment an employee earns based on sales.   (   )

[ambiguously, collect, commission, hush, scholarship,
stand a chance, swagger, that is]

Q4. Choose the most suitable word or phrase from the list above to fill in the blanks. If necessary, correct the word form.

1. We have a big competition three days from now, (   ), on Friday.

2. He went to drama school on a (   ).

3. Over a million donations have been (   ).

4. (   ) now and try to sleep.

5. He (   ) into the room looking very pleased with himself.

6. It was an (   ) worded agreement.

7. You get a 10 per cent (   ) on everything you sell.

8. The driver didn't (   ) of stopping in time.

UNIT **9**

Warm Up

Recite the following sentences out loud.

1. They had a bad quarrel and didn't make it up for a week.
2. He can't get rid of the headache.
3. It was only to get people's attention that they bought the company.
4. It turned out that she was a friend of my sister.
5. What an amazing view it is!

They did not make it up, Preacher and Billy Bob; and it was not because they didn't want to, it was only that there did not seem to be any straight way for their friendship to happen again. But they couldn't get rid of this friendship: each was always aware of what the other was up to; and when Preacher found himself a new buddy, Billy Bob moped around for days, picking things up, dropping them again, 5 or doing sudden wild things, like purposely poking his finger in the electric fan. Sometimes in the evenings Preacher would pause by the gate and talk with Aunt El. It was only to torment Billy Bob, I suppose, but he stayed friendly with all of us, and at Christmas time he gave us a huge box of shelled peanuts. He left a present for Billy Bob, too. It turned out to be a book of Sherlock Holmes; and on the flyleaf there 10 was scribbled, "Friends Like Ivy On The Wall Must Fall." That's the corniest thing I ever saw, Billy Bob said. Jesus, what a dope he is! But then, and though it was a cold winter day, he went in the backyard and climbed up into the pecan tree, crouching there all afternoon in the blue December branches.

But most of the time he was happy, because Miss Bobbit was there, and she was 15 always sweet to him now. She and Sister Rosalba treated him like a man; that is to say, they allowed him to do everything for them. On the other hand, they let him win at three-handed bridge, they never questioned his lies, nor discouraged his ambitions. It was a happy while. However, trouble started again when school began. Miss Bobbit refused to go. "It's ridiculous," she said, when one day the principal, Mr. Copland, 20

NOTES

line

1 **make it up**「仲直りする」

2 **it was only that ~**「ただ~というだけだった」

3 **happen**「~が起こる」この場合は友情が元どおりになること。

3 **get rid of**「なしにする」

4 **up to** = doing（話）「おこなって」

5 **buddy**「仲間、相棒」

5 **moped around** > mope around「ふてくされる、うじうじする」

6 **wild things** > wild thing「無茶なこと」

6 **poking** > poke [poʊk]「突く、突っこむ」

6 **electric fan**「扇風機」

7 **would**（過去の反復的動作）「よく~した（ものだ）」

8 **torment**「痛めつける、ひどく悩ませる」

9 **shelled peanuts**「殻をむいたピーナッツ」shelled「殻を取った」。

10 **turned out** > turn out「（~だということが）分かる、判明する」

10 **flyleaf**「（書籍の巻頭や巻末の）白紙」

11 **scribbled**「走り書きされた」scribble（動）の過去分詞。

11 **ivy**「つた、アイビー」

11 **corniest**　corny（話）（形）「ひどく感傷的な、陳腐な」の最上級。

12 **Jesus**（間投詞）「驚いた、ちくしょう」

12 **dope**（俗）「ばか、とんま」

13 **crouching** > crouch「かがむ、うずくまる」

16 **sweet**（形）「（人が）親切な、やさしい」

16 **a man**「（子どもではなく）大人の男」

17 **allowed him to**　allow A to「A が~するのを許可する」

18 **three-handed bridge**「三人でするブリッジ」bridge はトランプでおこなうゲーム。通常は二人または四人で行う。

18 **discouraged** > discourage [dɪsˈkʌrɪdʒ]「（希望などを）くじく、水をさす」

20 **refused** > refuse「拒否する」

20 **ridiculous** [rɪˈdɪkjələs]「こっけいな、ばかげた」

20 **the principal**（名）「校長」principal は団体の長、または主役など。

came around to investigate, "really ridiculous; I can read and write and there are *some* people in this town who have every reason to know that I can count money. No, Mr. Copland, consider for a moment and you will see neither of us has the time nor energy. After all, it would only be a matter of whose spirit broke first, yours or mine. And besides, what is there for you to teach me? Now, if you knew anything 25 about dancing, that would be another matter; but under the circumstances, yes, Mr. Copland, under the circumstances, I suggest we forget the whole thing." Mr. Copland was perfectly willing to. But the rest of the town thought she ought to be whipped. Horace Deasley wrote a piece in the paper which was titled "A Tragic Situation." It was, in his opinion, a tragic situation when a small girl could defy what he, for 30 some reason, termed the Constitution of the United States. The article ended with a question: *Can she get away with it?* She did; and so did Sister Rosalba. Only she was colored, so no one cared. Billy Bob was not as lucky. It was school for him, all right; but he might as well have stayed home for the good it did him. On his first report card he got three F's, a record of some sort. But he is a smart boy. I guess he just couldn't 35 live through those hours without Miss Bobbit; away from her he always seemed half-asleep. He was always in a fight, too; either his eye was black, or his lip was split, or his walk had a limp. He never talked about these fights, but Miss Bobbit was shrewd enough to guess the reason why. "You are a dear, I know, I know. And I appreciate you, Billy Bob. Only don't fight with people because of me. Of course they say mean 40 things about me. But do you know why that is, Billy Bob? It's a compliment, kind of. Because deep down they think I'm absolutely wonderful."

21　**investigate**「調査する、取り調べる」

21　**there are _some_ people in this town** ～「この町には～するひとがいる」some がイタリックで、「（実際に）いる」ことが強調されている。

22　**have every reason to**「～するあらゆる理由がある、申し分なく～できる」

23　**consider for a moment and** ～「すこし考えてみてください、そうしたら～」命令文 + and ～の表現。

23　**the time nor energy**「（この問題についやす）時間も労力も」neither ～ has A nor B「～のどちらも A も B もない」。

24　**would**（仮定に対する）「～だろう」

24　**broke**　仮定法過去。「もし校長先生と私がこのことで争うことになったら、どちらの心が先に折れるか」という仮定の話。

25　**besides**「その上、～に加えて」

25　**if you knew ～, that would ….**「もしあなたが～を知っているなら、…でしょう」仮定法過去。

26　**another matter**「またちがった話」

26　**under the circumstances**「こういう事情なので」

27　**I suggest**「～を提案します、～するのがよいでしょう」

28　**willing to**「～して構わない、～するのに特に異存がない」

28　**whipped** > whip（動）「むちで打つ」の過去分詞。受動態。

29　**a piece**　ここでは an article と同義。「記事」。

29　**tragic**「悲劇的な、なげかわしい」

30　**defy** [dɪˈfaɪ]（動）「～に公然と反抗する、平然と無視する」

30　**for some reason**「なんらかの理由で」語り手は皮肉でこう述べている。

31　**termed** > term（動）「～と名付ける、～と呼ぶ」

31　**the Constitution of the United States**「合衆国憲法」

32　**get away with it**「（悪事などを）うまくやる、～の罰を逃れる」

32　**so did Sister Rosalba** > so did A「A もまたそうした」

32　**only**（話）（接続詞的用法）「ただしかし～」

33　**It was school for him, all right**「学校とは彼のためのものだったのだ、まさに」この時代、特に南部では、学校は中流階級の白人、そして主に男子のためにあり、Bill Bob は学校に通わなくてよいとはみなされなかった、ということ。

34　**might as well**「～したほうがよい」

34　**good** = benefit（名）「役立つこと、ためになること」

34　**report card**「成績表」

35　**F's**（米）「（成績評価で）不可、落第」= failure.

35　**a record of some sort**「一種の記録ではあるけれど」

36　**away from her**「彼女と離れていると」副詞句。

37　**either his eye was black**「彼のどちらかの目のまわりは黒くなっていた」けんかをして殴られたことを示す。

38　**limp**（名）「足を引きずること」

38　**shrewd** [ʃruːd]（形）「鋭い、洞察力のある」

39　**dear**（名）「いい人、やさしい人」

39　**appreciate** [əˈpriːʃɪeɪt]（動）「よさをわかっている、真価を理解する」

41　**compliment**（名）「賛辞、誉め言葉」

42　**deep down**「（心の）奥底では」

EXERCISES

Q1. Choose the most suitable word to each blank in the following summary from the word list blow.

Billy Bob and Preacher (1) each other but cannot seem to find a way to become friends again. Preacher leaves Christmas presents for Billy Bob's family and for Billy Bob. Billy Bob feels sad and miserable about his (2) friendship with Preacher, but he is also happy, because Miss Bobbit and Rosalba are (3) to him. Miss Bobbit refuses to attend school because she is only interested in studying (4). People in town become upset that she is not forced to go to school. Billy Bob goes to school but (5) his classes. He gets into fights defending Miss Bobbit.

[kind, fails, dance, lost, miss]

Q2. Mark the following sentences true (T) or false (F) according to the story. If it's false, correct it.

1. The friendship between Preacher and Billy Bob is soon forgotten by both of them.

[   ]

2. Preacher replaces Billy Bob with a new friend. [   ]

3. Preacher gives peanuts to Billy Bob's family and a book to Billy Bob for Christmas.

[   ]

4. Billy Bob soon forgets about Preacher and is happier without him. [   ]

5. Miss Bobbit refuses to go to school because they won't let Rosalba attend.

[   ]

6. Billy Bob has to go to school, but he is a terrible student. [   ]

7. Miss Bobbit is upset by the newspaper article and the town gossip about her.

[   ]

8. Billy Bob gets into fights because people are gossiping about Preacher. [   ]

Q3. Match definition 1–8 with the appropriate word or phrase below.

1. to cause a person or animal to suffer.   (   )
2. to end an argument with somebody and become friends again.   (   )
3. to refuse to obey or show respect for somebody in authority.   (   )
4. to recognize the value of someone.   (   )
5. to write something quickly and carelessly.   (   )
6. the basic principles that a country is governed by.   (   )
7. a comment that expresses praise or approval of somebody.   (   )
8. occupied with; doing.   (   )

[appreciate, compliment, constitution, defy,
make it up, scribble, torment, up to]

Q4. Choose the most suitable word or phrase from the list above to fill in the blanks. If necessary, correct the word form.

1. Your kindness and generosity is much (   ).
2. Throughout the interview the journalists (   ) away furiously.
3. It's a great (   ) to be asked to do the job.
4. Numbers of workers have (   ) the president's decision.
5. I have no idea what she's (   ) these days.
6. Your right to vote is secured by the (   ).
7. She was (   ) by her bad memories.
8. Have those two (   ) yet?

UNIT **10**

Warm Up

Recite the following sentences out loud.

> 1. The professor is very much admired by his students.
> 2. He took the trouble to show me around town.
> 3. I have no idea what you mean.
> 4. Am I right in thinking that you'll support us?
> 5. He didn't come home until eleven o'clock.

And she was right: if you are not admired no one will take the trouble to disapprove. But actually we had no idea of how wonderful she was until there appeared the man known as Manny Fox. This happened late in February. The first news we had of Manny Fox was a series of jovial placards posted up in the stores around town: Manny Fox Presents the Fan Dancer Without the Fan; then, in smaller print: Also, 5 Sensational Amateur Program Featuring Your Own Neighbors—First Prize, A Genuine Hollywood Screen Test. All this was to take place the following Thursday. The tickets were priced at one dollar each, which around here is a lot of money; but it is not often that we get any kind of flesh entertainment, so everybody shelled out their money and made a great to-do over the whole thing. The drugstore cowboys talked 10 dirty all week, mostly about the fan dancer without the fan, who turned out to be Mrs. Manny Fox. They stayed down the highway at the Chucklewood Tourist Camp; but they were in town all day, driving around in an old Packard which had Manny Fox's full name stenciled on all four doors. His wife was a deadpan pimento-tongued redhead with wet lips and moist eyelids; she was quite large actually, but compared 15 to Manny Fox she seemed rather frail, for he was a fat cigar of a man.

They made the pool hall their headquarters, and every afternoon you could find them there, drinking beer and joking with the town loafs. As it developed, Manny Fox's business affairs were not restricted to theatrics. He also ran a kind of employment bureau: slowly he let it be known that for a fee of $150 he could get for 20

NOTES

line

1 **she**「ミス・ボビット」

1 **if you are not admired … to disapprove.** 尊敬されているからこそあえて非難されるような意味。

1 **trouble**「迷惑、面倒、手数」

2 **disapprove**「(…を) 非とする；(…に) 不賛成である」

2 **had no idea of … until~**「~して初めて…と思った」

3 **Fox**「フォックス」fox「狐 (きつね)」には、「狡猾 (こうかつ) な人」の意味もあり、「ずる賢い」(sly) イメージがある。

4 **a series of**「一続きの」

4 **jovial**「陽気な、楽しい、愉快な、快活で面白い」

4 **placard**「はり紙、掲示、ポスター」アクセント注意 /plǽkɑɚd/

4 **posted** > post「(ビラなど) をはる、掲示する」

5 **town**「(無冠詞)(話者の付近の、または、現在住んでいる) 町、都市」

5 **Manny Fox Presents … Without the Fan** と **Also, … A Genuine Hollywood Screen Test.** フォックスのポスターの文言を示す (ただし「then, in smaller print:」は除く)。

5 **Fan Dancer** > fan dance「ファンダンス《大きな扇を使って踊るソロのヌードダンス》」

6 **sensational**「すばらしい」

6 **Amateur**「素人の」/ǽmətʃùɚr/ 発音注意。

6 **Featuring** > feature「(映画・番組などが)(俳優など) を主演 (主役) とする」

7 **Genuine**「正真正銘の」

7 **Hollywood Screen Test**「ハリウッド映画のオーディション」

7 **All this was to take place** この was は動詞ではなく、助動詞 (auxiliary verb) で、be + to 不定詞の形で、「予定・命令・義務・運命・可能・目的」などを表し、ここでは予定を示す。

7 **take place**「行われる」

9 **flesh entertainment**「扇情的な余興 (公演)」flesh (名)「(人などの) 肌」

9 **shell out**「(…に)〈金〉を (しぶしぶ) 支払う (for, on)」

10 **to-do**「大騒ぎ」

10 **over** = about

10 **drugstore cowboy** = the regular customers who gossip all day

10 **cowboy** いわゆる「カウボーイ」ではなく、俗語で「乱暴者、悪漢」

11 **talked dirty** > talk dirty「淫らに話す」dirty は副詞。

12 **highway**「幹線道路」

12 **Tourist Camp**「旅行者宿泊 (収容) 施設」

13 **Packard**「パッカード」同社名 (名門高級車メーカー) の車。

14 **stenciled** > stencil「型板で (模様・文字など) を (…に) 刷る」

14 **deadpan**「無表情な、ポーカーフェイスの」

14 **pimento-tongued** = using spicy language

15 **redhead**「赤毛の人」

16 **frail**「弱々しい、ひ弱な、かよわい」

16 **a fat cigar of a man**「太い葉巻のような男」(名詞 +of+ 名詞の語順で、後の名詞が前の名詞のようであることを示して)、しばしば同じ意味を形容詞で表わすことができる。an angel of a girl (= an angelic girl)「天使のような少女」

17 **pool hall** = pool room「賭け玉突き場」

18 **loafs** > loaf「浮浪者、ごろつき」=loafer. 食品の loaf ではない。

any adventurous boys in the county high-class jobs working on fruit ships sailing from New Orleans to South America. The chance of a lifetime, he called it. There are not two boys around here who readily lay their hands on so much as five dollars; nevertheless, a good dozen managed to raise the money. Ada Willingham took all she'd saved to buy an angel tombstone for her husband and gave it to her son, and 25 Acey Trump's papa sold an option on his cotton crop.

21　**adventurous**「大胆な；進取の気性に富んだ」

21　**county**「(アメリカの) 郡」州 state の中では最大の行政区画、ただし2州を除く。

21　**fruit ships**「果物運搬船」

22　**the chance of a lifetime**「またとないよい機会」

23　**readily**「たやすく、難なく (easily)」

23　**lay their hands on** > lay (one's) hands on「…を手に入れる、自分ものにする (obtain)」

23　**so much as**「(普通は否定語の後で) …さえ (≒ even)」She didn't mention it in so much as a whisper.
「彼女は一言もそれに言及しなかった」

24　**good**「(a ~ として) たっぷり (まる) …分の」

24　**raise**「(金) を集める」

25　**angel tombstone**「嘆きの天使の彫刻付きの墓石」

26　**option**「オプション、選択売買権 (一定期間内に定められた価格で売買する権利) (on)」

"placard" (p. 54, l. 4)

文字通り「プラカード」とすると、デモ行進のときに掲げる「プラカード」を連想しますが、ここでは、「はり紙、掲示、ポスター」の意味です。

　以下、和製英語を列挙してみました。英語としては通じない和製英語から英語の特徴を考えてみましょう。

　「ミシン」は machine から来ており、英語では sewing machine となります。

　「ワイシャツ」は、white shirt が訛ったと言われ、shirt あるいは dress shirt (礼装用) であり、下着の「シャツ」は undershirt となります。

　「ノートパソコン」は、英語では laptop PC で、机上に置いて容易に移動しない desktop PC に対します。

　「サイン」は、文書などの署名であれば signature、有名人に求めるものであれば autograph となります。

　「クレーム」で混同しやすいのは、英語の claim は確かにあります。それは単に「主張する」意味になります。例えば、They claimed (to have won) the victory.「勝ったと主張した」というような。日本語で使われている「苦情」の意味とは異なります。日本語の意味を英語で伝えるなら、complain, complaint となります。

　「コンセント」も consent で英語でもありそうですが、電源を取る差込口を「コンセント」というのは concentrical plug に由来する和製英語です。consent では assent, agree などの同義語で「承諾、同意」の意味しかありません。電源の差込口を意味したいなら、米国では outlet、英国では socket と呼ばれます。「コンセントにつなぐ」は plug in です。

　「レンジ」だと「範囲」の意味の range で、たしかにレンジの意味もありますが、アメリカでは cooking stove「調理用レンジ」の方が普通です。「電子レンジ」は、microwave (oven) となります。さらに「チンする」だと、microwave を動詞で使うか、zap, nuke などという言い方もあります。もちろん温め、加熱の意味で heat something in a microwave で OK です。

Q1. Choose the most suitable word to each blank in the following summary from the word list blow.

A stranger named Manny Fox comes to town. He (1) a show. The show includes a dance performance by Mrs. Manny Fox and a talent contest that anyone can (2). First prize in the talent contest is a Hollywood Screen Test. Even though the tickets are expensive, everyone (3) one. Manny Fox also has an employment business. For a fee of $150, he (4) to find a good job on a fruit ship. This is a lot of money, but about a dozen families manage to (5) the fee.

[enter, pay, advertises, promises, buys]

Q2. Mark the following sentences true (T) or false (F) according to the story. If it's false, correct it.

1. "If you are not admired, no one will take the trouble to disapprove" is the explanation provided by the narrator for why the townspeople disapproved of Miss Bobbit.

[   ]

2. The narrator also disapproves of Miss Bobbit. [   ]

3. "The drugstore cowboys talk dirty all week." This line means the men in town who gather to gossip at the drugstore expect the dance to be sexy. [   ]

4. The fan dance performance is advertised on the radio. [   ]

5. Manny's wife is frail. [   ]

6. Manny Fox offered to find good jobs for boys because he wanted to help the town.

7. The narrator believes the jobs are a "chance of a lifetime." [   ]

8. Ada Willingham used her savings to pay for her son to get a job on a fruit boat.

[   ]

Q3. Match definition 1–8 with the appropriate word or phrase below.

1. make extra effort. ( )

2. physically weak and thin. ( )

3. to pay money for something, often unwillingly. ( )

4. great in number, amount or degree. ( )

5. willing to take risks, brave. ( )

6. real; exactly what it appears to be. ( )

7. an amount of money that you pay for something. ( )

8. a place from which an organization is controlled, home office. ( )

[adventurous, fee, frail, genuine, good,
headquarters, shell out, take trouble]

Q4. Choose the most suitable word or phrase from the list above to fill in the blanks. If necessary, correct the word form.

1. This is a ( ) picture by Millet.

2. The firm's ( ) are in London.

3. It took me a ( ) ten hours to finish it.

4. Mother was becoming too ( ) to live alone.

5. The job was dangerous so only ( ) people applied.

6. Please ( ) to read the introduction and footnotes.

7. The band ( ) $100,000 for a mobile recording studio.

8. "How much is the admission ( )?" "4,500 yen for an adult and 2,500 yen for a child."

UNIT **11**

the 22nd paragraph

32

Warm Up

Recite the following sentences out loud.

> 1. We got a twenty-year mortgage on our house.
> 2. Harry is washing the dishes in the sink.
> 3. She gave away all her party dresses.
> 4. They're distant relatives of mine.
> 5. They had to contend with cultural differences.

33   But the night of the show! That was a night when all was forgotten: mortgages, and the dishes in the kitchen sink. Aunt El said you'd think we were going to the opera, everybody so dressed up, so pink and sweet-smelling. The Odeon had not been so full since the night they gave away the matched set of sterling silver. Practically everybody had a relative in the show, so there was a lot of nervousness to contend   5 with. Miss Bobbit was the only contestant we knew real well. Billy Bob couldn't sit still; he kept telling us over and over that we mustn't applaud for anybody but Miss Bobbit; Aunt El said that would be very rude, which sent Billy Bob off into a state again; and when his father bought us all bags of popcorn he wouldn't touch his because it would make his hands greasy, and please, another thing, we mustn't be   10 noisy and eat ours while Miss Bobbit was performing. That she was to be a contestant had come as a last-minute surprise. It was logical enough, and there were signs that should've told us; the fact, for instance, that she had not set foot outside the Sawyer house in, how many days? And the victrola going half the night, her shadow whirling on the window shade, and the secret, stuffed look on Sister Rosalba's face whenever   15 asked after Sister Bobbit's health. So there was her name on the program, listed second, in fact, though she did not appear for a long while. First came Manny Fox, greased and leering, who told a lot of peculiar jokes, clapping his hands, ha, ha. Aunt El said if he told another joke like that she was going to walk straight out: he did, and she didn't. Before Miss Bobbit came on there were eleven contestants, including   20

NOTES

line

1 **mortgage**「(抵当を入れてする) 借金、(特に) 住宅ローン」発音注意 /mɔ́ːɡɪdʒ/ で、t は発音しない。

3 **pink**「感動した、興奮した」動詞といっしょだと get (turn) pink 英語では健康・若さ・純真などを象徴し、日本語の「ピンク」のように性的な意味合いはない。そのような場合はしばしば blue を用いる。blue「(口語) 猥褻 (わいせつ) な、下品な (obscene)」blue jokes「きわどい冗談」

3 **sweet**「香りのよい」音が sweet であれば「耳に快い」

3 **The Odeon**「オデオン座」Paris の Théâtre de l'Odéon に倣って。(一般に) 音楽堂、劇場。odeon = odeum「(古代ギリシア・ローマの) 奏楽堂」

4 **give away**「配る、安く売る (distribute)」

4 **matched**「そろいの」= uniform, same design.

4 **sterling silver**「純銀」

5 **relative**「親類」

5 **contend with**「競う、張り合う」

6 **contestant**「(競技会などの) 出場者」

7 **still**「静かに、動かないで」

7 **over and over (again)**「何度も何度も」

7 **applaud**「(劇・演技・出演者など) に拍手する (clap hands, cheer)」

7 **but**「(no (one), nothing, anything, all, everybody, anywhere, who, where などの後で) …を除いて、…のほかは (≒ except).」

8 **that** = applauding only for Miss Bobbit.

8 **rude**「不作法な、失礼な、無礼な (impolite)」

8 **sent ... off** > send ...off「(人) をぼーっとさせて (〜に) する」

8 **state**「(通例 in [into] a 〜で) 興奮 (神経質な) 状態」

9 **would**「(否定文で強い主張・拒絶などを表わす) どうしても…しようとしなかった」ex. The patient just wouldn't take any medicine. その患者はどうしても薬を飲もうとしなかった。

9 **his** = his bag of popcorn

10 **greasy**「脂でよごれた」

11 **That she was to be a contestant** = 主部。ここでの was to be の形は、be + to do の形で、(予定を表わし) …することになっている、…する予定だ」の意味。他に義務、可能、運命なども示すことがある。

12 **signs**「(…の) 前兆、徴候、きざし」

13 **set foot**「立ち入る」

15 **window shade**「(米) ブラインド (≒ blind)」

15 **stuffed** = an exclamation of contemptuous anger or annoyance, especially against another person.

16 **listed** > list 日本語の「リストアップ」は和製英語。英語では listing といい、「リストアップする」は make a list of または list という。

18 **greased** > grease「(髪に) 油 (グリース) を塗る」

18 **leering**「(人が) 横目を使う、いやらしい目つきの」

18 **peculiar**「(不快なふうに) 妙な、変な」

18 **clapping** > clap「(手) をたたく」

19 **straight**「率直に、正直に:あからさまに」

20 **contestant**「競演者」

Eustacia Bernstein, who imitated movie stars so that they all sounded like Eustacia, and there was an extraordinary Mr. Buster Riley, a jug-eared old wool-hat from way in the back country who played "Waltzing Matilda" on a saw. Up to that point, he was the hit of the show; not that there was any marked difference in the various receptions, for everybody applauded generously, everybody, that is, except Preacher Star. He was sitting two rows ahead of us, greeting each act with a donkey-loud boo. Aunt El said she was never going to speak to him again. The only person he ever applauded was Miss Bobbit. No doubt the Devil was on her side, but she deserved it. Out she came, tossing her hips, her curls, rolling her eyes. You could tell right away it wasn't going to be one of her classical numbers. She tapped across the stage, daintily holding up the sides of a cloud-blue skirt. That's the cutest thing I ever saw, said Billy Bob, smacking his thigh, and Aunt El had to agree that Miss Bobbit looked real sweet. When she started to twirl the whole audience broke into spontaneous applause; so she did it all over again, hissing, "Faster, faster," at poor Miss Adelaide, who was at the piano doing her Sunday-school best. "I was born in China, and raised in Jay-pan . . . " We had never heard her sing before, and she had a rowdy sandpaper voice. ". . . if you don't like my peaches, stay away from my can, o-ho o-ho!" Aunt El gasped; she gasped again when Miss Bobbit, with a bump, up-ended her skirt to display blue-lace underwear, thereby collecting most of the whistles the boys had been saving for the fan dancer without the fan, which was just as well, as it later turned out, for that lady, to the tune of "An Apple for the Teacher" and cries of gyp gyp, did her routine attired in a bathing suit. But showing off her bottom was not Miss Bobbit's final triumph. Miss Adelaide commenced an ominous thundering in the darker keys, at which point Sister Rosalba, carrying a lighted Roman candle, rushed onstage and handed it to Miss Bobbit, who was in the midst of a full split; she made it, too, and just as she did the Roman candle burst into fiery balls of red, white and blue, and we all had to stand up because she was singing "The Star Spangled Banner" at the top of her lungs. Aunt El said afterwards that it was one of the most gorgeous things she'd ever seen on the American stage.

22 **jug-eared**「（水差しの取っ手のように）大きな耳の」

23 **back country**「（米）奥地、僻（へき）地」

23 **"Waltzing Matilda"**「ウォルツィング・マティルダ」オーストラリアの国民歌で、邦題「旅にはスワッグ (swag) をもって」swag は、「（豪）（放浪者・坑夫などの携帯する）身のまわり品の包み」Matilda は女性名マティルダだが、豪俗語で「マティルダ（山地旅行者・放浪者らが身の回り品を入れて持ち歩く細長い包み）」その原義は、mighty in battle で、熟語 walk (waltz) Matilda は「自分の包みを携帯して放浪する、荷物一つで渡り歩く」

23 **saw**「のこ（ぎり）、鋸」musical saw とか singing saw と呼ばれる楽器の一種。

24 **receptions** > reception「（世間の）受け、反応」

26 **boo**「（人に）ブーといってやじる、ブーイングを浴びせる」

29 **tossing** > toss「（頭などを）ぷいと上げる、つんとそらす（軽蔑・いらだち・自尊心・気概などの表現）」

29 **curls** > curl「（髪の）カール、巻き毛」

30 **classical**「クラシックの、古典派の」日本語の「クラシック」は「古典音楽」の意だが、英語では classical music といい、英語の classic はギリシャ・ローマ時代のことをいう。

30 **daintily**「優美に、上品に、繊細に」

32 **smacking** > smack「（…を）ぴしゃりとたたく、ひっぱたく」

33 **spontaneous**「自発的な、任意の；（態度などが）自然な；（よい意味で）（人が）自ら進んでする」

34 **hissing** > hiss「（…ということを）小声できつく（怒りを込めて）言う」

35 **Sunday-school**「日曜学校（宗教教育のために教会などで日曜日に開かれる学校）」Miss Adelaide usually plays piano for children in church.

35 **Jay-pan** > Japan

36 **rowdy**「（人が）騒々しい；乱暴な、けんか好きな」

37 **peaches** > peach「（俗）乳房、おっぱい」

37 **stay away**「近づかない、ちょっかいを出さない」

37 **can**「（俗）ミルク缶」つまり「（俗）おっぱい (breasts)」

37 **o-ho**「（驚き・愚弄（ぐろう）・歓喜などを表わして）おほー！、ほーっ！、おや！」

37 **gasp**「（恐怖・驚きで）息をのむ、息が止まる」

38 **bump**「（俗）バンプ（腹や腰を急に前に突き出す挑発的な踊り方）」cf. bumps and grinds「ストリップ・ダンサーの腰を突き出したり回したりする動作」ここは、with a bump「どんと、どしんと」ではない。

41 **"An Apple for the Teacher"**「先生にりんごを」apple-polish「（人の）ごきげんをとる、（人に）ごまをする」なので、「先生にゴマすり」ということ。apple-polish の語源は、米国の学童が先生にぴかぴかに磨いたリンゴを贈った風習からと言われる。

41 **gyp** > gee up の派生語。gee「はいはい（馬を急がせる掛け声）」で、Gee up! はいはい (Gee-up)！ 逆に制止する掛け声は、whoa.

42 **bathing suit**「水着」

43 **commence** = begin, start.

43 **darker keys** > dark key「黒鍵」

44 **Roman candle**「ローマ花火、筒形花火（円筒の中に火薬を入れたもので、手に持って揚げる；吹き出る火花の中から時々火の玉が飛び出る）」

45 **split**「両脚を開いて一直線にする形（演技）」

45 **made it** > make it「うまくいく、成功する」

47 **"The Star Spangled Banner"**「星条旗」ここは、米国国歌。もちろん国旗 stars and stripes の意味にもなる。

47 **at the top of her lungs** > at the top of one's lungs「声を限りに」

EXERCISES

Q1. Choose the most suitable word to each blank in the following summary from the word list blow.

The night of the show, the theater is crowded. Everyone is (1) up. Miss Bobbit has been secretly practicing her dance for days. Billy Bob is (2) as he waits for her to perform. Preacher boos all of the (3) except Miss Bobbit. Miss Bobbit surprises the audience by performing a mature dance and (4) her underpants. She (5) as well as dances and ends her performance with "The Star Spangled Banner."

[dressed, showing, sings, performers, nervous]

Q2. Mark the following sentences true (T) or false (F) according to the story. If it's false, correct it.

1. Mortgages and dishes in the sink are examples of why some people could not go to the show.   [   ]

2. Billy Bob is excited at the beginning of the show because Miss Bobbit is going to perform.   [   ]

3. Only a few people sign up to perform in the show.   [   ]

4. Everyone knows that Miss Bobbit has been practicing for the show all week.

[   ]

5. The narrator respects and admires Manny Fox.   [   ]

6. Before the show, Rosalba seems to be the only one who knows exactly what Miss Bobbit has planned for her performance.   [   ]

7. Aunt El becomes angry with Preacher because he boos all the performers except Miss Bobbit.   [   ]

8. Aunt El is shocked by Miss Bobbit's poor skill as a dancer.   [   ]

Q3. Match definition 1–8 with the appropriate word or phrase below.

1. again.   (   )

2. a dance move, sitting down with legs straight out on either side of the body.

                                                                   (   )

3. not planned, impulsive, unintentional.   (   )

4. someone who enters a contest, often to perform.   (   )

5. careful, often in a way that suggests good manners; delicate.   (   )

6. to slap or hit with force.   (   )

7. a sound that people make to show that they do not like a performer.

                                                                   (   )

8. to applaud, to praise with your hands.   (   )

[boo, clap, constant, dainty, over, spontaneous, split, smack]

Q4. Choose the most suitable word or phrase from the list above to fill in the blanks. If necessary, correct the word form.

1. The audience cheered and (   ).

2. It's all wrong—you'll have to do it (   ).

3. The dancer did the (   ) on stage twice.

4. She took a (   ) little bite of the apple.

5. She (   ) her hand down on the table.

6. The audience burst into (   ) applause.

7. The unpopular speech was greeted with loud (   ) from the audience.

8. All the (   ) were nervous before the show.

UNIT **12**

the 23rd & 24th paragraphs

Warm Up
34

Recite the following sentences out loud.

> 1. A nuclear war cannot be won.
> 2. He looks as if he's given up.
> 3. We'll skip the exercise.
> 4. Her hands were trembling with cold.
> 5. He could not bring himself to report her to the police.

Well, she surely did deserve a Hollywood screen test and, inasmuch as she won
35
the contest, it looked as though she were going to get it. Manny Fox said she was:
honey, he said, you're real star stuff. Only he skipped town the next day, leaving
nothing but hearty promises. Watch the mails, my friends, you'll all be hearing from
me. That is what he said to the boys whose money he'd taken, and that is what he   5
said to Miss Bobbit. There are three deliveries daily, and this sizable group gathered
at the post office for all of them, a jolly crowd growing gradually joyless. How their
hands trembled when a letter slid into their mailbox. A terrible hush came over them
as the days passed. They all knew what the other was thinking, but no one could
bring himself to say it, not even Miss Bobbit. Postmistress Patterson said it plainly,   10
however: the man's a crook, she said, I knew he was a crook to begin with, and if I
have to look at your faces one more day I'll shoot myself.

Finally, at the end of two weeks, it was Miss Bobbit who broke the spell. Her
36
eyes had grown more vacant than anyone had ever supposed they might, but one day,
after the last mail was up, all her old sizzle came back. "O.K., boys, it's lynch law   15
now," she said, and proceeded to herd the whole troupe home with her. This was the
first meeting of the Manny Fox Hangman's Club, an organization which, in a more
social form, endures to this day, though Manny Fox has long since been caught and,
so to say, hung. Credit for this went quite properly to Miss Bobbit. Within a week
she'd written over three hundred descriptions of Manny Fox and dispatched them to   20

NOTES

line

1 **she** = Miss Bobbit

1 **inasmuch as**「…であるから (≒ since, because)」

2 **the contest**   Manny Fox が主催したコンテストのこと。

2 **as though** / as if「(seem, look などとともに) …のようだ」

2 **it** = the Hollywood screen test

2 **she was** > she was going to get the Hollywood screen test

3 **stuff**「素質、才能、才」

3 **only**「しまいには、結局は」

3 **skipped** > skip「(町などを) こっそり去る；…から逃亡する (flee)」

6 **sizable**「相当の大きさの、かなり大きい (fairly large)」

7 **jolly** = merry「しあわせな、期待でいっぱいの」

8 **tremble**「(恐怖・怒りなどで) 震える (shiver, shudder)」

8 **slid** > slide

8 **hush**「静寂；沈黙」

10 **bring himself** > bring oneself to do「(cannot を伴って) …する気になる」

10 **not even Miss Bobbit** = even Miss Bobbit could not bring herself to say it.

10 **Postmistress**「女性郵便局長」postmaster の女性形。

11 **the man's** = the man (= Manny Fox) is

11 **crook** [krʊk]「悪人、犯罪者 (criminal)；詐欺師 (con man)」

11 **to begin with**「そもそも」

12 **shoot myself** > shoot oneself「ピストルで自殺する」

13 **it**   強調構文の主語として、it is … that 節または wh 節の形で。It was Jill who (that) spoke first.「最初に口をきいたのはジルでした (Jill spoke first. の Jill を強調)」

13 **broke the spell** > break a (the) spell「まじないを解く；迷夢をさます」

14 **vacant**「ぽかんとした、うつろな (absentminded)」

14 **they might** = Miss Bobbit's eyes might grow vacant

15 **up**「終わって (over)；だめで」

15 **sizzle** = determination, energy (as if it had boiling heat).

15 **lynch law**「私刑、リンチ (絞首などによる非合法な処刑)」

16 **herd**「(人) を (追い) 集める、移動させる」

16 **troupe** [tru:p]「(俳優・歌手などの) 一座、一団 (company, band) 」

17 **the Manny Fox Hangman's Club**「マニー・フォックスを絞首刑にする会」cf. hangman「絞首刑執行人」

18 **endure**「持ちこたえる、存続する (≒ last)」

18 **long since**「ずっと前に」

19 **so to say**「言わば、さながら (as it were)」

19 **credit**「名誉、手柄、功績、称賛」

19 **properly**「当然のことながら」

20 **descriptions** > description「人相書」

20 **dispatch**「…を急送する」

Sheriffs throughout the South; she also wrote letters to papers in the larger cities, and these attracted wide attention. As a result, four of the robbed boys were offered good-paying jobs by the United Fruit Company, and late this spring, when Manny Fox was arrested in Uphigh, Arkansas, where he was pulling the same old dodge, Miss Bobbit was presented with a Good Deed Merit award from the Sunbeam Girls of America. 25 For some reason, she made a point of letting the world know that this did not exactly thrill her. "I do not approve of the organization," she said. "All that rowdy bugle blowing. It's neither good-hearted nor truly feminine. And anyway, what is a good deed? Don't let anybody fool you, a good deed is something you do because you want something in return." It would be reassuring to report she was wrong, and that her just 30 reward, when at last it came, was given out of kindness and love. However, this is not the case. About a week ago the boys involved in the swindle all received from Manny Fox checks covering their losses, and Miss Bobbit, with clodhopping determination, stalked into a meeting of the Hangman's Club, which is now an excuse for drinking beer and playing poker every Thursday night. "Look, boys," she said, laying it on the 35 line, "none of you ever thought to see that money again, but now that you have, you ought to invest it in something practical—like me." The proposition was that they should pool their money and finance her trip to Hollywood; in return, they would get ten percent of her life's earnings which, after she was a star, and that would not be very long, would make them all rich men. "At least," as she said, "in this part of the 40 country." Not one of the boys wanted to do it: but when Miss Bobbit looked at you, what was there to say?

21 **papers**「(一般的に) 新聞 (社)」

23 **the United Fruit Company**「ユナイテッド・フルーツ (社)」現在の「チキータ・ブランド」(Chiquita Brands International)。

24 **Arkansas**「アーカンソー (米国中南部の州)」発音注意 /ɑ́ɚkənsɔ̀ː/

24 **dodge**「(いかがわしい) 商売、仕事」

25 **a Good Deed Merit award**「善行功労賞」

25 **the Sunbeam Girls of America**「全米サンビーム・ガールズ」あえて訳せば、「全米栄光若年女性団体」救世軍の一部、ガールスカウトに似た団体。

26 **made a point of** > make a point of「…を強調 (重視) する、懸命に (念を入れて、わざわざ) …する」

27 **the organization** = the Sunbeam Girls of America

27 **rowdy**「(人が) 騒々しい；乱暴な、けんか好きな」

27 **bugle**「(軍隊の) らっぱ；ビューグル (trumpet より小さいらっぱでバルブはない)」

32 **swindle**「詐取、詐欺、ぺてん (fraud)」

33 **checks** > check「小切手」

33 **clodhopping** = blunt「無作法な」

34 **stalked** > stalk「威張って歩く」

35 **laying it on the line** > lay it on the line「(言いにくいことを) はっきり言う」

36 **now that**「(今はもう) …であるから、…となった今 (以上) は」

37 **proposition**「(商売・政治上の) 提案、提言、申し入れ；企画」

40 **which … would make them all rich men**「彼女がスターになれば、そしてそれは遠い先のことではないのだが、みんなお金持ちになるだろう」投資などしたくないけど、ボビットの一睨みで言いなりになる男の子たちが描かれている。また、would は仮定を表す。

"Hangman" (p. 66, l. 17)

この hangman「絞首刑執行人」は、hanger とも言い換えられ、hanger はまた、衣服をかける「ハンガー」でもあります。語源から言えば、Old English の「揺れる、ためらう」に遡ります。

日常生活ではついお手軽に服をハンガーにかけてしまいますが、着物用の衣紋掛けがあるものの、以前はたたむ方がふつうだったでしょう。「たたむ」は fold で「畳」に象徴されるように、たたむ文化は日本の大きな特徴です。

古代の「畳」は、莚・莫蓙・菰などの薄い敷物の総称で、使用しないときは「畳」んで部屋の隅に置いたことから、動詞の「たたむ」が名詞化して「畳」になったのが語源とされます。

団扇 (うちわ) をたためば、扇子 a folding fan になるし、衝立をたためば、a folding screen 屏風になります。他にも、折りたたみ式ベッド a folding bed、折りたたみ椅子 (腰掛け) a folding chair (stool) や折り尺 a folding rule (scale) もありますし、そして何よりも、折り紙 the art of paper folding があります。海外で、手土産代わりに、鶴を折る fold origami paper into a crane ことでもできれば、拍手喝采は疑いないでしょう。

折り紙の応用技術が、宇宙開発でも重宝されています。例えば、衛星の限られたスペースに太陽光パネルをコンパクトに収納し、容易に展開が可能となったことはよく知られていますが、日本語の「畳」の語源を思わせます。

Q1. Choose the most suitable word to each blank in the following summary from the word list blow.

Miss Bobbit wins the contest easily, and Manny Fox tells her that she's a real star. The next day Manny Fox leaves town, saying only that they should all (1) for mail. Everyone waits eagerly for mail from Manny Fox. Finally, the woman who works for the post office tells them that Manny Fox is obviously a thief and con artist. They have all been (2). Miss Bobbit organizes the Manny Fox's Hangman's Club. She sends out descriptions of Manny Fox to over 300 sheriffs and also sends letters to newspapers. Manny Fox is caught and (3) in the spring. The boys who were cheated of $150 all receive checks. Miss Bobbit asks the boys to (4) their money in her Hollywood career. She promises to make them rich, and they are afraid to (5) her.

[invest, refuse, cheated, arrested, watch]

Q2. Mark the following sentences true (T) or false (F) according to the story. If it's false, correct it.

1. Manny Fox leaves town after the show without a word to anyone.　　　[　]

2. Miss Bobbit is the only one who waits to hear from Manny Fox.　　　[　]

3. Manny Fox sent messages three times a day to the boys and Miss Bobbit. [　]

4. The "terrible hush" that falls over the townspeople is because they are afraid they have been cheated by Manny Fox.　　　[　]

5. The phrase "all her old sizzle came back" refers to Miss Bobbit's energy and determination.　　　[　]

6. The first meeting of the Manny Fox Hangman's Club is at the boarding house where Miss Bobbit and her mother live.　　　[　]

7. Manny Fox is hung for his crimes.　　　[　]

8. The boys in the Manny Fox Hangman's Club are eager to finance Miss Bobbit's trip to Hollywood to become a star.　　　[　]

Q3. Match definition 1–8 with the appropriate word or phrase below.

1. happy and cheerful. (   )
2. a dishonest person; criminal. (   )
3. excitement, passion, determination. (   )
4. make a special and noticeable effort to do something. (   )
5. empty, empty of expression. (   )
6. considering that; since. (   )
7. to deal with something painful or unpleasant without giving up; bear.

(   )
8. to do something worthy of reward or punishment. (   )

[crook, deserve, endure, inasmuch, jolly, make a point of, sizzle, vacant]

Q4. Choose the most suitable word or phrase from the list above to fill in the blanks. If necessary, correct the word form.

1. That salesman is a real (   ).
2. The child (   ) a prize for her performance.
3. He was a (   ) man full of jokes.
4. She (   ) taking a walk each day.
5. His (   ) eyes lifted to stare out into the distance.
6. They had to (   ) a long wait before the case came to trial.
7. It was not really a still life (   ) as all the objects were in motion.
8. We live in an age that values (   ) more than substance, so all news stories must be exciting.

UNIT **13**

Warm Up

Recite the following sentences out loud.

> 1. Heavy water sinks and buoyant water rises.
> 2. There wasn't much sun today.
> 3. She was hot and sweat dripped into her eyes.
> 4. She scuttled off when she heard the sound of his voice.
> 5. She remained dry-eyed throughout the trial.

Since Monday, it has been raining buoyant summer rain shot through with sun, but dark at night and full of sound, full of dripping leaves, watery chimings, sleepless scuttlings. Billy Bob is wide-awake, dry-eyed, though everything he does is a little frozen and his tongue is as stiff as a bell tongue. It has not been easy for him, Miss Bobbit's going. Because she'd meant more than that. Than what? Than being thirteen 5 years old and crazy in love. She was the queer things in him, like the pecan tree and liking books and caring enough about people to let them hurt him. She was the things he was afraid to show anyone else. And in the dark the music trickled through the rain: won't there be nights when we will hear it just as though it were really there? And afternoons when the shadows will be all at once confused, and she will pass 10 before us, unfurling across the lawn like a pretty piece of ribbon? She laughed to Billy Bob; she held his hand, she even kissed him. "I'm not going to die," she said. "You'll come out there, and we'll climb a mountain, and we'll all live there together, you and me and Sister Rosalba ..." But Billy Bob knew it would never happen that way, and so when the music came through the dark he would stuff the pillow over his 15 head.

Only there was a strange smile about yesterday, and that was the day she was leaving. Around noon the sun came out, bringing with it into the air all the sweetness of wisteria. Aunt El's yellow Lady Anne's were blooming again, and she did something wonderful, she told Billy Bob he could pick them and give them to Miss Bobbit for 20

NOTES

line

1 **buoyant**「軽快な、快活な、うきうきした (cheerful)」用例としては、in a buoyant mood ルンルン気分で、buoyant force 浮力など。語源は float の意味から。

1 **shot** > shoot「〈光線など〉を発する」すぐ前の rain を修飾する。

1 **sun**「日光 (sunshine)」太陽 (the sun) ではない。

2 **dripping** > drip = (of liquid) to fall in small drops.

2 **leaves** > leaf「木の葉」

2 **chimings** > chime「(鐘・チャイムが) 鳴る」ここでは、雨音が鐘の音のように聞こえる、ということ。

3 **scuttlings** > scuttle「急いで行く (hurry along)、あわてて走る (scurry)」。ここでは動物かなにかが眠らずに動いている、ということ。

3 **wide-awake**「すっかり目をさました」例えば、She was wide awake when the burglar broke in. そのどろぼうが侵入してきた時彼女はすっかり目がさめていた。

3 **dry-eyed**「(人が) 泣いていない (not crying)」いわゆる「乾き目、ドライアイ」ではない。

4 **frozen**「無感動の、感情を失った (paralyzed, numb)」

4 **tongue** = clapper「(鐘・鈴の) 舌 (ぜつ)」

4 **It** = Miss Bobbit's going

5 **that** = Miss Bobbit's going

6 **queer**「妙な、奇妙な、奇態な、風変わりな (odd)」クィア理論 (queer theory) は、性や性同一性に関する伝統的な考え方に疑問を呈し、これを改めようとする文化・文芸批評理論である。

6 **pecan**「ペカン (米国中・南部産のくるみ科の木)」発音注意 /píːkæn/

7 **caring … about** > care for「が好きだ、を好む (≒ like)」

8 **trickled** > trickle「したたる、ぽたぽた落ちる」

10 **afternoons**　前に won't there be を補う。

10 **all at once**「突然、不意に (≒ suddenly)」

10 **shadows**「影法師たち」Miss Bobbit が「光」として、他の者たちを「影」としている。

10 **she will pass**　前に afternoons when を補う。

11 **unfurling** > unfurl「(光景を) 眼前に繰り広げる、見せる (unfold)」

11 **She laughed to Billy Bob … and Sister Rosalba …**　ビリー・ボブの妄想。

14 **that way**「そんなふうに (like that)」

15 **stuff**「(物を) 押し込む、突っ込む (thrust, press)」

17 **Only there was a strange smile about yesterday …** = The townspeople were happy for Miss Bobbit, even though they are sad to see her leave.

19 **wisteria**「フジ (マメ科フジ属 (Wisteria) の植物の総称)」

19 **blooming** > bloom「花が咲く、開花する」名詞でも使うが、bloom は、ばら・チューリップ・菊など、主に観賞するための花を指し、blossom は、りんご・みかんなど、特に実を結ぶ花を指す。周知の flower は、この bloom と blossom とを包摂する上位語である。

good-bye. All afternoon Miss Bobbit sat on the porch surrounded by people who stopped by to wish her well. She looked as though she were going to Communion, dressed in white and with a white parasol. Sister Rosalba had given her a handkerchief, but she had to borrow it back because she couldn't stop blubbering. Another little girl brought a baked chicken, presumably to be eaten on the bus; the only trouble was she'd forgotten to take out the insides before cooking it. Miss Bobbit's mother said that was all right by her, chicken was chicken; which is memorable because it is the single opinion she ever voiced. There was only one sour note. For hours Preacher Star had been hanging around down at the corner, sometimes standing at the curb tossing a coin, and sometimes hiding behind a tree, as if he didn't want anyone to see him. It made everybody nervous. About twenty minutes before bus time he sauntered up and leaned against our gate. Billy Bob was still in the garden picking roses; by now he had enough for a bonfire, and their smell was as heavy as wind. Preacher stared at him until he lifted his head. As they looked at each other the rain began again, falling fine as sea spray and colored by a rainbow. Without a word, Preacher went over and started helping Billy Bob separate the roses into two giant bouquets: together they carried them to the curb. Across the street there were bumblebees of talk, but when Miss Bobbit saw them, two boys whose flower-masked faces were like yellow moons; she rushed down the steps, her arms outstretched. You could see what was going to happen; and we called out, our voices like lightning in the rain, but Miss Bobbit, running toward those moons of roses, did not seem to hear. That is when the six-o'clock bus ran over her.

22 **stopped by** > stop by = make a short visit somewhere

22 **wish**「（well (ill) を伴って）（人に）（よかれと）祈る」We all wish you well.「皆あなたのことをよかれと思っている」

22 **Communion**「（プロテスタント）聖餐（せいさん）式、（カトリック）聖体拝領 (Holy Communion)」キリストが最後の晩餐で、パンと葡萄酒をとり、「これわがからだなり、わが血なり」と言ったことに基づいて、パンと葡萄酒を会衆に分かつ儀式。洗礼式とともに、キリスト教でもっとも重要視される。

24 **blubbering** > blubber「泣きわめく、おいおい泣く、泣きじゃくる」

27 **by**「…に関して（は）、…について（は）」That's fine by me.「私はそれで結構です」

31 **It** 前文全体。Preacher Star の態度、様子のこと。

31 **sauntered** > saunter「散歩する、ぶらつく、歩き回る」

33 **heavy**「（程度などが）激しい、強い」

36 **bouquets** > bouquet「ブーケ、（手に持つ）花束」発音注意 /boʊkéɪ, bu:-/

37 **bumblebees of talk**「マルハナバチのようなにぎやかな話のざわめき」bumblebee 自体は、「（昆虫）マルハナバチ」で羽音が大きい。形式的には、（名詞 + of + a + 名詞で）「…のような」用法としては、前の部分の名詞 + of が形容詞の役割をする」an angel of a boy「天使のような少年」

37 **talk**「（世間の）話 (report)；うわさ（話）、風説 (rumor, gossip)」

38 **yellow**「Lady Anne という薔薇の黄色」

40 **call out**「大声で叫ぶ、呼び求める」

41 **the six-o'clock bus ran over her** 冒頭の一文が Yesterday afternoon the six-o'clock bus ran over Miss Bobbit. であったことを思い出そう。

"wisteria" (p. 72, l. 19)

日本の「藤」に当たる花で、花言葉 (the language of flowers) は、「歓迎」、「確固たる、しっかりした、忠実な」など。その後、Bob が Bobbit に渡そうとする黄色い薔薇は「友情」（他にもいくつか）を示します。

　花 (flower) 全体として「儚さ（はかな）」を象徴することは周知のとおりです。聖書の「イザヤ書」(Isaiah) 40 章 7–8 節には、「人は草、……草は枯れ、花は萎（しぼ）むが、わが神の御言葉は永遠なり」とあり、ヘリック (Robert Herrick, 1591–1674) は「乙女たちに、時を惜しめ」(To the Virgins, to Make Much of Time, 1648) の冒頭で「薔薇の蕾を摘もう、そうできるうちに、／時の翁はいつもたちまち過ぎ去る」(Gather ye rose-buds while ye may, / Old Time is still a-flying) と詠んでいます。

　これは俗に言う carpe diem (= seize the day)「命短し恋せよ乙女」の主題で、その意味は、「（将来を憂えず）今を楽しめ」とか、「（二度と戻らぬ）この瞬間を大切に生きよ」になります。

　志村喬 (1905–82) 主演の《生きる》(1952) で最後に「いのちみじかし、こいせよおとめ」で始まる「ゴンドラの唄」(1915) を口ずさみます。

　ロビン・ウィリアムズ (Robin Williams, 1951–2014) 主演の《いまを生きる》(Dead Poets Society, 1989) は、原題通りだと《死せる詩人の会》ですが、主人公 John Keating 先生の carpe diem という言葉をタイトルにしています。

EXERCISES

Q1. Choose the most suitable word to each blank in the following summary from the word list blow.

Billy Bob is heartbroken. He knows he will probably never (1) Miss Bobbit again after she goes to Hollywood. The day Miss Bobbit plans to leave, people in town visit her and wish her good luck. Preacher shows up and (2) around to say good-bye to Miss Bobbit. Billy Bob cuts roses to give to Miss Bobbit before she leaves town. Preacher and Billy Bob (3) the flowers into two bouquets to present to Miss Bobbit. When Miss Bobbit sees the two boys holding roses, she (4) toward them. As she crosses the street, the bus comes. People call out to (5) her, but she doesn't seem to hear. The bus runs over her, and Miss Bobbit dies.

[waits, warn, see, divide, rushes]

Q2. Mark the following sentences true (T) or false (F) according to the story. If it's false, correct it.

1. Billy Bob is excited that Miss Bobbit is getting her chance to go to Hollywood.

   [   ]

2. Billy Bob knows that he will never see Miss Bobbit again once she leaves town.

   [   ]

3. The narrator thinks Billy Bob is a foolish 13-year-old boy who will soon forget his first love.   [   ]

4. The narrator believes they will all miss Miss Bobbit when she leaves town, not just Billy Bob.   [   ]

5. Many people stopped at the boarding house to say goodbye to Miss Bobbit.

   [   ]

6. Miss Bobbit's mother finally speaks to reject the chicken offered to her.   [   ]

7. Preacher and Billy Bob seem to forgive each other at the end of the story. [   ]

8. Miss Bobbit runs in front of the bus because she is excited to leave town. [   ]

Q3. Match definition 1–8 with the appropriate word or phrase below.

1. suddenly.   (   )

2. cry noisily.   (   )

3. make a short visit.   (   )

4. walk in a slow relaxed way; stroll.   (   )

5. run with quick short steps; scurry.   (   )

6. express strong desire or hope.   (   )

7. go somewhere slowly or gradually.   (   )

8. yelling, shouting.   (   )

[all at once, blubber, call out, saunter, scuttle, stop by, trickle, wish]

Q4. Choose the most suitable word or phrase from the list above to fill in the blanks. If necessary, correct the word form.

1. I'll (   ) this evening for a chat.

2. People began (   ) into the hall.

3. There he sat, (   ) like a baby.

4. We (   ) them both well in their retirement.

5. She (   ) off when she heard the sound of his voice.

6. He (   ) by, looking as if he had all the time in the world.

7. She (   ) to him as he passed on the bike.

8. But (   ), in the midst of his happy life came tragedy.

TRUMAN CAPOTE
Children on Their Birthdays
詳注詳解　カポーティの「誕生日の子どもたち」

著　者	Truman　Capote
編注者	Karen　Mcgee
	植　月　惠一郎
	松　浦　恵　美
発行者	山　口　隆　史

発 行 所　　　株式会社 音羽書房鶴見書店

〒113-0033　東京都文京区本郷 3-26-13
TEL 03-3814-0491
FAX 03-3814-9250
URL: https://www.otowatsurumi.com
e-mail: info@otowatsurumi.com

2023 年 3 月 1 日　　初版発行
2024 年 3 月 15 日　　2 刷発行

組版　ほんのしろ
装幀・イラスト　田中希実
印刷・製本　（株）シナノ パブリッシング プレス
■ 落丁・乱丁本はお取り替えいたします。　　　　F-080